# NO GREATER SAVIOR

RICHARD LEE
ED HINDSON

**HARVEST HOUSE PUBLISHERS**
Eugene, Oregon 97402

**NO GREATER SAVIOR**

Copyright © 1995 by Harvest House Publishers
Eugene, Oregon 97402

Library of Congress Cataloging-in-Publication Data

Lee, Richard, 1944–
    No greater savior / Richard Lee, Ed Hindson.
      p.  cm.
    ISBN 1-56507-265-0
    1. Jesus Christ—Meditations.    I. Hindson, Ed., 1944– .    II. Title.
BT306.4.L425     1994                                  94-29308
232—dc20                                                CIP

**Printed in the United States of America.**

95  96  97  98  99  00  01  —  10  9  8  7  6  5  4  3  2  1

*To all sincere seekers after Jesus Christ*
*who wish to know Him better.*

# Contents

**Part Three:**
*What Manner of Man Is This?*

**Part Four:**
*Surely This Is the Son of God!*

# Preface

Jesus Christ is the greatest person who has ever lived. There is no one greater. There is no one who even begins to compare with Him. His person. His character. His wisdom. His love. He outshines them all!

There have been great men and women whose lives have made an impact while they were here on earth. But the greatest of them does not hold a candle to the blazing brilliance of this one life. He stands like a mountain of granite against the sands of the seashore by comparison.

It is our sincere hope that you will come to know Him better as you feel His presence in the pages of this book. Walk with Him on the grassy hillsides of Galilee. Sail with Him across the lake. Travel with His disciples as they traverse the hills and valleys of Judea. Stand with Him in the Temple. Listen as He teaches. Follow Him to Gethsemane. Linger among the olive trees as you watch Him there in prayer.

Each chapter in the pages ahead is a verbal picture of the Savior. Together they paint a portrait of Jesus of Nazareth. What was He really like? Why did so many people believe He was the Messiah? Could He really heal the sick and raise the dead? Was He truly the Savior of the world?

As you read, let Jesus speak to you personally. Let the magnitude of His person and the power of His presence fill your soul with the wonder of Him . . . and Him alone.

—Richard Lee
Ed Hindson
*There's Hope!*
Atlanta, GA

*Jesus is more ready to pardon than you are to sin,*
*More willing to supply your wants*
*Than you are to confess them.*
*Never tolerate low thoughts of Him.*
*You may study, look, and meditate,*
*But Jesus is a greater Savior than you think Him to be*
*When your thoughts are at their highest.*

Charles H. Spurgeon

# Part One

# Who Could This Be?

*Come, see a man who told me everything I ever did. Could this be the Christ?*

—John 4:29

# 1
~

# A Love Like
No Other

*When Christ came into the world, he said: "Sacrifice and offering you did not desire, but a body you prepared for me. . . . I have come to do your will, O God."*
Hebrews 10:5,7

Every child knows the opening lines of Clement Moore's famous poem, "Twas the Night Before Christmas." It conjures up visions of the arrival of a special visitor. It throws us back into the happy days of our childhood dreams. The very imagery of the poem makes us joyful with anticipation. We cannot wait for the one who is coming.

Have you ever wondered what *really* happened the night before the *first* Christmas? Before the shepherds came? Before the wise men arrived? Even before the innkeeper sent Joseph and Mary to the stable?

The Bible gives us a glimpse into heaven itself on the night before that Christmas. Strangely, our text is not found in the Gospels, but in the book of Hebrews. There, the author tells us what went through the mind of Christ as He prepared to come into the world of mankind. Quoting Psalm 40:6-8 as the words of Christ, the Scripture states emphatically: "When Christ came into the world, he said: '. . . a body you prepared for me. . . . I have come to do your will, O God'" (Hebrews 10:5,7).

The sacrificial system of Old Testament religion had ceased to meet God's requirements. It was never intended to be permanent. From the very beginning, it pointed to a *final and eternal sacrifice*. Even on the night of the first Passover, the blood of the lamb signified a greater sacrifice yet to come. After the lambs were slain, their blood was collected in buckets which were taken to the people's homes. With the bucket of blood at their feet, the children of Israel dipped in their sponges and reached up to smear the blood over the top of the door-posts. Then, they reached from side to side to cover the sideposts. In the process, they were making the sign of the *cross!*

It was a picture of what would come later as a result of Christ's coming to earth.

We can only imagine what the angels must have thought about all of this. "Is He actually going there?" they must have wondered. "They don't even deserve Him," some may have responded. "At least we didn't fall for Satan's silly lies," others may have said. "They're so undeserving! Satan took them captive so easily and so quickly!"

The Bible simply tells us: "Concerning this salvation . . . even angels long to look into these things" (1 Peter 1:10,12). Surely we can assume they were mystified by Christ's deliberate choice to be made "lower than the angels" (Hebrews 2:9). What an unthinkable decision!

"Lower than us?" The angels must have thought. "Why would He do such a thing?"

He was the Son of God, seated on the throne of heaven. The Scripture says, "The Son is the radiance of God's glory and the exact representation of his being . . . at the right hand of the Majesty in heaven" (Hebrews 1:3). Why would He leave that high and lofty place? Why would He step down from His exalted position? Why would He risk an incarnation? Why would He bother with Christmas?

The simple answer is . . . He did it for us! We do not deserve it and we dare not try to explain it. *The only explanation is grace.*

Hundreds of years before His birth, God the Father said, "You are my Son. . . . Ask of me, and I will make the nations your inheritance, the ends of the earth your possession" (Psalm 2:7-8). The writer of Hebrews explains this transaction as "bringing many sons to glory" (2:10).

Yes, Jesus was temporarily made lower than the angels by His incarnation. But ultimately, He was "crowned with glory and honor . . . so that by the grace of God he might taste death for everyone" (Hebrews 2:9).

The only explanation the Bible offers for Christmas is that He did it for us. He was God's gift to all mankind. He came to suffer and die for our sins. He came to take the punishment we deserved. He gave Himself that we might go free. What a Savior!

Charles Wesley expressed it best when he wrote:

> Amazing love! How can it be
> That Thou, my God, shouldst die for me![1]

Whether the angels were surprised by Christmas we can only guess. But once the decision was made, they were quick to announce its details. Their message came not as a proclamation of judgment, but as a declaration of joy. And heaven's joy it was!

"I bring you good news of great joy," the angel told the shepherds. "A Savior has been born to you" (Luke 2:10-11). He was not born for Himself. He was born for others. He was born that He might bring us to glory.

He who was the eternal God, higher than the angels, was made lower than the angels, that we who were lower than the angels might be made higher than the angels. *In Christ we become more than we ever deserved to be.* Higher than the angels! We are precious in His sight, secure in His love, and elevated by His grace. He has done for us what we cannot do for ourselves. He has made us children of God, adopted us into the family of God.

No one ever loved you like Jesus loves you! He set His love on you before He ever left heaven to come to earth. He came to set you free. To claim you as His own... that you might touch the face of God.

Who can resist such love? Reach out to Him by faith. If you can trust Him for eternity, you can trust Him to meet your needs today. ✳

# 2

## Before the Angels Sang

*The one who comes from above is above all; the one who is from the earth belongs to the earth, and speaks as one from the earth. The one who comes from heaven is above all.*

John 3:31

Long before Joseph and Mary made their difficult journey to Bethlehem, Micah 5:2 had predicted: "But as for you, Bethlehem... from you One will go forth for Me to be ruler in Israel. His going forth are from long ago, from the days of eternity" (NASB).

This raises some intriguing questions: Where was Jesus prior to being laid in the manger? What was He doing before Gabriel's announcement to Mary? Where was He before the choir of angels sang to the shepherds on the night of His birth?

The Bible answers those questions with this sweeping declaration: "In the beginning was the Word, and the Word was with God, and the Word was God" (John 1:1). Jesus Christ, the Son of God, the Savior of the world, had always existed from all eternity. He is the same essence and quality as the Father and the Spirit. He is and has always been the eternal God.

*There is no greater Savior!* Jesus alone is greater than all because He alone is eternal. He alone is God. Oxford theologian Alister McGrath states, "Jesus is God—that is the basic meaning of the incarnation. It is a remarkably profound and exciting idea which has enormous consequences for the way in which we think about ourselves and about God."[2]

McGrath explains that while God is infinite, immortal, and invisible, all that we know of Him personally is revealed in Jesus Christ. Jesus alone is God in visible form. Not only is Christ God-like, but God is Christ-like! Until Christ came, every image of God that was conceived by man was made in the form of man or beast. It was merely an idol. But in Christ we see the image of God in human flesh.

Jesus is deity on foot! He walks among men, but He lives above men. He looks like a man, but He talks like God. He is fully human and yet totally divine. He is the *window* through which we see the nature and character of God in action. And He is the *mirror* through which we see ourselves in relation to God.

When Jesus' own disciple, Philip, insisted, "Lord, show us the Father," Jesus responded, "Don't you know me, Philip...? Anyone who has seen me has seen the Father" (John 14:8-9). There can be no doubt that Jesus clearly understood who He was and why He was here. He had come to reveal the true and living God. He was the *shekinah* glory veiled in a robe of human flesh. He was indeed the embodiment of the power and presence of God on earth.

John's Gospel begins by calling our attention to the greatness of Jesus Christ. He is greater than all in His *Person* because He is the incarnation of the infinite and eternal God. He has always existed and He will always exist. His very being is coexistent with the Father. He is one and the same with God.

Jesus is also greater than all in His *power*. He is the Creator. "All things were made" by Him and "in Him was life" (John 1:3-4). He alone is the source of life. He is the One who gives meaning and purpose to His creation. The universe itself is ample testimony to His creative power. It is the repository of His greatness. No wonder the psalmist sings, "The heavens declare the glory of God; the skies proclaim the work of His hands" (19:1).

Our Lord is also greater than all in His *promise*. John opens his Gospel by reminding us that Jesus alone can make us sons of God by faith in Him. "Yet to all who received him, to those who believed in his name, he gave the right to become children of God" (John 1:12). We are not God's children by natural birth; we must be adopted into His family. And Jesus alone promises to make that transaction for us.

Christ is also greater than all in His *priority*. He alone is the preexistent Son of God incarnate in human flesh. John the apostle said of Christ, "The Word became flesh and lived for a while among us. We have seen his glory, the glory of the one and only Son, who came from the Father, full of grace and truth" (John 1:14). What a testimony! Jesus alone personifies the glory of God Almighty. He is God visible and in person.

Finally, John points out through the words of John the Baptist that Jesus is greater than all in His *purpose*. "Look, the Lamb of God," the Baptist proclaimed, "who takes away the sin of the world!" (John 1:29). Jesus did not come to earth just to be a teacher, although He was a teacher. He did not come merely to set a better example, even though He did set a better example.

Ultimately, He came to die for our sins. That was His greatest purpose.

The Lord explained this in detail to Joseph when He reassured him of the divine and miraculous nature of Mary's child. "She will give birth to a son," He said, "and you are to give him the name Jesus, because he will save his people from their sins" (Matthew 1:21).

*Yeshua.* Jesus. Savior.

What a perfect name! What a perfect Savior!

We cannot consider the life and message of Jesus without coming face to face with greatness. As you gaze into these glimpses of His person and His teaching, you will encounter *Him.* Time and time again, you will have to ask yourself: How is my relationship to Him?

Jesus is no mere person. And knowing Him is no casual relationship. The very magnitude of His being overwhelms us. His wisdom, power, love, and compassion overcome the skepticism in all of us. And the greatness of His teaching overshadows anything we have ever heard before.

There is no greater Savior! ❋

# 3

# The Silence Is Broken

*W*hile they were there, the time came for the baby to be born, and she gave birth to her firstborn, a son. She wrapped him in strips of cloth and placed him in a manger, because there was no room for them in the inn.

Luke 2:6-7

A baby's cry broke the silence of the cool night air. And in that simple cry, the greatest turning point in human history unfolded.

The cry broke the silence of God.

God had been silent for 400 years. He had not uttered a word since the days of the prophets. His people had stopped listening, so God stopped talking. For four centuries, no matter how desperately Israel pleaded, there was no word from God.

The Old Testament ended with a terrible and deafening thud. Malachi, the last of the prophets, wrote, "I will send you the prophet Elijah. . . . He will turn the hearts of the fathers to their children, and the hearts of the children to their fathers; or else I will come and strike the land with a curse."

From that time onward, centuries passed in which Gentile armies brutally occupied the towns and villages of Israel. Messianic hopes peaked and faded countless times. And still, Elijah did not come—only the Roman legions did. Brute force ruled the land and smashed the people's dreams of a new king, like David. Surely they were under the curse of God!

Yet there were those who refused to give up hope. Some people still believed that God would intervene. Somehow. Some way. The long-awaited King of Israel would appear! God would once again smile upon His people! Somehow. Some way. God would break His silence and speak again.

But a baby's cry? Four hundred years of divine silence ended with an infant's wail? Only God could have orchestrated such a scene.

Bethlehem was crowded with visitors. There was no room for Mary and Joseph in the inn. The stable, cut out of a cave in the rocks nearby, served as a shelter for the young couple. It was warm and private. But it was still a barn!

The scene boggles the mind. The Messiah in a manger? With animal attendants? Wrapped in a blanket? Lying in the straw? Who could have imagined such a thing?

God!

The Creator of the universe honored His creation by sending His incarnate Son into the most humble of circumstances. Jesus' birth dignified God's creation and minimized man's achievements. The very scenery of that night shouts to us of God's grace.

The King of kings was born in a barn that none might despair. The humblest and lowest person on earth could find hope in such a Savior. Slaves were born better than this—but God chose to send His Son into the world as a display of His grace to *all* men.

The Bible profoundly states, "For you know the grace of our Lord Jesus Christ, that though he was rich, yet for your sakes he became poor, so that you through his poverty might become rich" (2 Corinthians 8:9).

*The birth of Jesus broke the long silence of God.* In the humble surroundings at Bethlehem, the King of Israel had been born. A direct descendant of David, born in the City of David—but born in a barn. Nothing could have been more appropriate. God had sent His Son into the world to reveal Himself to *all* men, regardless of status, circumstance, or position.

The divine incarnation lay helpless that night in His mother's arms. All He could do was cry . . . but that cry signaled the turning point of history. God had come back!

Divine hope lit up the stable. The Light of the world had burst into the darkness of that night. Divine revelation resounded in a baby's crying. The Way, the Truth, and the Life had come to offer hope and salvation to mankind.

Jesus would later weep over Jerusalem and sob at the tomb of Lazarus. He would moan over our sin and groan over its application to His sinless soul. He would weep over our pain and cry out to God for our deliverance.

The baby who broke the silence of God that night with His cries in the manger would become our great Savior. He is our High Priest who offers up "prayers and petitions with loud cries and tears" (Hebrews 5:7). The crying baby has become the weeping Savior who intercedes on our behalf!

Jesus is crying for you. Think of it! Whatever your heartaches may be, He has a heart for your deepest sorrows. When your soul cries out to Him, He hears with tears in His eyes. He is touched with the feeling of your hurts. He is moved with love and compassion to heal your broken heart.

The baby's cry in the manger was the word from God that the world had waited so long to hear. The silence was broken. God was speaking. The baby's cry was the Father insisting that He loved us!

Charles Spurgeon said, "There is more of God's glory and majesty to be seen in the manger than in the sparkling stars above, the rolling deep below, the towering mountain, or the teeming valley. . . . Let us then give ourselves up to holy wonder, such as will produce gratitude, worship, love, and confidence, as we think of that great mystery of godliness, God manifest in the flesh!"[3]

Jesus came to earth to bear the consequences of our sin and to prepare us to live with Him for all eternity. How ironic that the One who cried *for* us, and who now cries *with* us, will eventually cry *no more.* And neither shall we! Revelation 21:4 promises: "He will wipe every tear from their eyes. There will be no more death or mourning or crying or pain, for the old order of things has passed away."

God is calling. Are you listening? ✳

# 4

~

# The Glory Returns

*nd there were shepherds living out in the fields nearby, keeping watch over their flocks at night. An angel of the Lord appeared to them, and the glory of the Lord shone around them, and they were terrified.*

Luke 2:8-9

Throughout Israel's long history, the glory of God was an ever-present reminder that He was with them. In the days of Solomon's Temple, the *shekinah* glory—the visible, awe-inspiring manifestation of His glory—filled the Holy of Holies. Only the high priest himself could enter that sacred room. And he could do it only *once* a year on the Day of Atonement (Yom Kippur). On that day atonement was made for the sins of the people as the high priest applied blood to the mercy seat of the Ark of the Covenant.

In that moment, the high priest stood in the presence of *God Himself*. Glory filled the room!

The sacredness of God barred the Jewish people from entering the Holy of Holies for any reason. Eventually they even tied a rope to the leg of the high priest before he entered. That way, they could pull him out from under the veil (or curtain) if he were to die while he was in the presence of God.

To stand in that room where the glory shone was the greatest privilege in all the world. Year after year, it was the highlight of the high priest's ministry. After much personal preparation, following all the prescribed laws of sanctification, he would begin that solemn journey into the presence of God.

But as the years rolled by, the people of Israel began to take His blessings for granted and rebel against His laws. Finally, after repeated attempts to call them to repentance, *God's glory departed.*

In the early days of the Babylonian invasion, the prophet Ezekiel testified that God's glory still resided on the Temple (Ezekiel 8:4). But Ezekiel also noted the pagan idols that had been placed in the Temple precincts (8:5,10) and the pagan practices that were tolerated there (8:14,16). The people of Israel had violated their covenant with God.

Gradually, reluctantly, but decisively, God's glory withdrew from the Ark of the Covenant (10:2), from the Holy of Holies (10:4), from the Temple itself (10:18). Finally, the glory departed from Jerusalem to the Mount of Olives. And from there it ascended back into heaven.

From that point on it was dark in the Holy of Holies. The glory was gone! *Ichabod!* The lights went out. The room was empty. God was not there!

We can only imagine what the high priest thought the next time he entered that sacred room. What's more, we can only imagine what he did.

No glory. No power. No God!

*I can't tell them that,* he probably thought. So, in

all likelihood, he came out of the darkness and lied to the people.

"I've seen the glory," he may had said. But really, he had seen nothing at all. He had to go on pretending God was still there when, in reality, all was dark.

Within a few years, the Babylonian army came and destroyed Jerusalem. The conquerors took Israel into captivity and wrecked the Temple. All the hopes and dreams of God's people were dashed.

Why did God let the Babylonians get away with it? Because He is not the curator of a religious museum. God was no longer in the Temple. The glory had departed!

The people prayed for God's glory to return, but it never did. Many years later, after the Babylonian captivity, the Jewish people returned to Jerusalem and built a second Temple. They prayed for God's glory to come upon it (Haggai 2:3), but there is no record in Scripture that God's glory ever returned.

For four centuries the people of Israel went through the motions of their religious rituals. They prayed. They cleansed. They sacrificed. They sanctified. But God was not there. The Holy of Holies remained dark. The glory did not return.

Israel's only hope in those dark days was Haggai's prophecy that God would one day fill that Temple with His glory (2:7-9). But for over 400 years that prophecy remained unfulfilled. The glory did not return.

Have you ever felt like you had lost the power and presence of God in your life? Do you feel that way now? Things just aren't the same anymore. You try to convince yourself that things are just fine, when they are not fine at all. The spark just isn't there anymore. You are empty and the lights are going out.

Don't give up hope! When the night is the darkest, dawn is just ahead. God will not turn a deaf ear to your prayers. It may seem like a long wait, but He will answer in His own—and perfect—time.

Remember that all seemed hopeless in Israel until that dark night outside the hills of Bethlehem when choirs of angels announced that *the glory had returned.* The angelic messenger was surrounded by the *shekinah* glory, the glory of God Himself. He had finally returned!

A host of angels sang His praises: "Glory to God in the highest, and on earth peace to men on whom his favor rests" (Luke 2:14). God had come to His people again and the hills were ablaze with His glory. R.C. Sproul writes, "The plains of Bethlehem became the theater for one of the most spectacular sound-and-light shows in human history."[4]

And to whom was this great news given? Shepherds! Where? At Bethlehem! Why? Because the Shepherd of Israel, David's Son, had come to claim His throne in power and glory. "Today in the town of David a Savior has been born to you; he is Christ the Lord," the angels proclaimed (Luke 2:11).

It was the greatest glory of all! It was the glory of God's presence incarnate in a newborn child. This time the glory was not hidden behind the veil of the Temple; this time it was on display in the *person* of Jesus Christ.

Martyn Lloyd-Jones observed, "Christianity is essentially something that concerns the person of the Lord Jesus Christ. We start with that fact and emphasize it, because Christianity is not primarily a teaching, nor a philosophy, nor even a way of life. In the first instance it is, before all, a relationship to a person."[5]

Jesus alone can light up your soul with the presence of God. ✳

# 5

## No Ordinary Child

*For my eyes have seen your salvation, which you have prepared in the sight of all people, a light for revelation to the Gentiles and for glory to your people Israel.*

Luke 2:30-32

When elderly people know they are nearing the end of the road of life, they tend to want to settle the important things. They also want some reassurances about the future—reassurances for that time after they are gone.

Such was the case with Simeon. He was a righteous and devout Jew who was looking expectantly for the coming of the Messiah. The Bible tells us that the Holy Spirit had revealed to him that he would not die until he had seen Him. But as the years passed and his age advanced, the old priest must have wondered if that day would ever come.

Suddenly, Simeon was "moved by the Spirit" to go out into the Temple courts. Could this be Him? But He was a baby, just eight days old! His parents had brought Him to the Temple to be circumcised according to the Law. They looked so poor and ragged. Yet, they were so humble, pure, and simple.

There could be no mistake—this was the One!

The aged priest took the baby in his arms and with great joy declared his readiness to depart in peace. He had seen the Savior! The glory had returned and the old man knew it. He praised God, blessed the child, and cautioned the parents: "This child is destined to cause the falling and rising of many in Israel," he announced (Luke 2:34). "Your own soul will be pierced," he warned Mary in particular, foreseeing the agony that was to come.

We know little of Jesus' childhood. The family apparently stayed in Bethlehem for a while. But the visit of the wise men stirred up such attention that they were forced to flee to Egypt to escape Herod's jealousy and wrath (*see* Matthew 2:11-23). Eventually, they returned to Nazareth in Galilee. There, near the lake, Jesus grew up in virtual obscurity, far from the tensions in Jerusalem.

Joseph, Jesus' earthly father, was a carpenter. Jesus probably learned this trade as a boy growing up in Nazareth. All we know for sure of His childhood is that His parents were devout Jews who went to Jerusalem every year for the Passover celebration.

When Jesus was 12 years old, an incident at the Temple gave a glimpse of things to come. The family traveled to Jerusalem (Luke 2:41) for the Passover that year with a large company of pilgrims. Upon their return home, Mary and Joseph assumed Jesus was somewhere in the group.

Since 12-year-old boys can be quite active, we should not be surprised that He was not missed. But by the end of the day they still had not seen Him. After a quick search, the parents realized Jesus was not with them and raced back to Jerusalem in panic. After three days, they finally found Him.

Why did it take three days? Where would you have looked for a 12-year-old? Running? Playing? Hiding? Not Jesus! He was in the Temple, "sitting among the teachers, listening to them and asking them questions" (Luke 2:46).

He was about His Father's "business," He called it. He expected His parents to understand—"Didn't you know I had to be in My Father's house?" He asked them. But the Bible explains, "They did not understand" (Luke 2:50). Nevertheless, Jesus obeyed them and returned home, where He "grew in wisdom and stature, and in favor with God and men" (Luke 2:52).

We know virtually nothing else about Jesus' childhood. All the rest is legend and speculation. The fact that He did not emerge in public until age 30 implies virtual obscurity over the next 18 years. Where He went, what He did, who He met—all is silent in Scripture. We can only assume that He attended the synagogue in Nazareth, studied Hebrew in the synagogue school, and learned His father's trade as a carpenter.

Still, as Josh McDowell so aptly put it, Jesus was more than a carpenter.[6] He never wrote a book, yet more books have been written about Him than any other person in history. He never traveled very far, yet more people have traversed the globe on His behalf than for any other person who has ever lived.

Even by secular standards, Jesus must be judged as the greatest and most influential person who has ever lived. The dates on our calendars and newspapers remind us daily that Jesus is the center of human history. The copyright on every university textbook bears witness to Jesus' influence on human society.

Even the brief glimpse we have of Jesus' childhood tells us *He was no ordinary child.* He upstaged everyone around Him. He upstaged Mary and Joseph at the manger. The shepherds came to see Him, not them. The wise men worshiped Him, not His parents. Herod tried to kill the baby, not the mother. The family fled to Egypt because of Him. Mary and Joseph went searching in Jerusalem because He was missing.

And even there, at the Temple, at age 12, He upstaged them all—His parents, the scholars, the rabbis. "Everyone who heard him was amazed," the Bible says (Luke 2:47). It is clear from this vignette that even at an early age He had a clear sense of who He was and why He was here.

Jesus returned home to Nazareth that day, but He would be back! He would return to the Temple—with a vengeance! Overturning the tables. Driving out the money changers. Scattering their precious coins. Stampeding the animals.

"Get out of here!" He would demand. "How dare you turn my Father's house into a market!" (John 2:16). Zeal for His Father's house would consume Him. The glory would come back, but Israel wouldn't be ready for Him.

That, however, was years in the future. Now, in Simeon's presence, he was a helpless infant—yet He was no ordinary child. Because He was no ordinary Savior. From the very beginning, His heart was fixed upon our salvation. He was determined to be about His Father's business... and that business was our redemption. ✳

# 6

## Family Ties

*S*omeone told him, *"Your mother and brothers are standing outside, wanting to speak to you." He replied to him, "Who is my mother, and who are my brothers?" Pointing to his disciples, he said, "Here are my mother and my brothers."*

Matthew 12:47-49

It wasn't easy growing up in Jesus' family. It had to be tough on the rest of them. After all, He was perfect. He never sinned.

How would you like to have been His brother or sister, living with a perfect child? No wonder they didn't understand Him—they could barely relate to Him.

Don't be surprised when you read that Jesus had brothers and sisters. Matthew 13:55 names the boys, (James, Joseph, Simon and Judas) and refers to the girls as His "sisters." Some people try to explain them away as "cousins," but the Bible makes it clear these were Joseph and Mary's children. They were born after the virgin birth of Christ and came via the more conventional route.

The Bible doesn't give us a lot of information on
Jesus' family, but their varied reactions to two separate
incidents stand out.

*Shock.* Mark tells us the family actually tried to stop
Him during His early ministry. Large crowds were
gathering to hear Him. He was casting out demons and
healing dozens of people, causing quite a stir in Galilee.

Mark 3:21 says, "When his family heard about this,
they went to take charge of him, for they said, 'He is
out of his mind.'" When they arrived, there was such an
enormous crowd they couldn't even get near Him. So
they sent someone into the house with a message that
they were there. "This is so embarrassing," one family
member may have said. "He's got to be stopped before
He makes a fool of Himself."

Eventually the messenger wiggled his way through
the crowd to Jesus. "Your mother and brothers are
standing outside, wanting to speak to you," he informed
Him.

"Here are my mother and my brothers," Jesus
said, referring to His disciples. That was His only reply.
Jesus was respectful; He never criticized his brothers or
sisters or belittled them. But He wasn't about to stop
His ministry to listen to their arguments, either. And
apparently they left, never getting the opportunity to see
Him.

*Denial.* The Scriptures say that Mary knew who
Jesus was from the beginning. But she often kept things
"in her heart" (Luke 2:51), rather than express them
openly. The Bible never implies that she did not believe
in Him.

However, that was not the case with his brothers.
John 7:5 says, "Even his own brothers did not believe in
him." Shocking? Not really. What if *your* brother

claimed to be the Messiah, God in human flesh? It
would be hard to believe.

John 7 tells us the Feast of Tabernacles was
approaching and Jesus' brothers urged Him to go to
Jerusalem. "Show yourself to the world," they urged
(verse 4). *How could He be the Messiah?* they must have
thought. *He won't even tell anyone who He is!*

Jesus' brothers simply couldn't comprehend His
ultimate purpose. For that matter, neither could
His own disciples, so we shouldn't be disappointed
at his brothers' response.

In fact, their disbelief underscores the credibility of
the biblical account. It speaks to us of reality. Of
honesty. Of transparency. Anyone wanting to portray
Jesus in an artificial, favorable light surely would have
said His brothers believed in Him. Yet the Bible says
they did not!

*Heartache.* In time, we can assume Jesus' family
grew distant from Him. Joseph is never mentioned after
the Temple incident when Jesus was 12. It is generally
assumed that Mary was widowed by the time Jesus began
His public ministry at age 30.

Eventually Jesus joined His brothers at the Feast of
Tabernacles and created a tremendous stir. Some people
claimed He was demon-possessed, while others wanted
to kill Him. Many believed He was the Messiah.

"When the Christ comes, will he do more
miraculous signs than this man?" they asked (John 7:31).
"Surely this man is the Prophet." Others agreed, "He is
the Christ" (verses 40-41). Even the Temple guards sent
to arrest Him came back empty-handed. "No one ever
spoke the way this man does," they admitted (verse 46).
Yet His own brothers did not believe in Him.

While Mary was present at the crucifixion, along
with her sister and several other women, there is no

reference to Jesus' brothers. In fact, Jesus entrusted Mary's care to His disciple, John (*see* John 19:25-27). As the eldest son, it was Jesus' responsibility to see that His widowed mother was properly taken care of. Interestingly, He did *not* leave her care to His own brothers.

*Hope.* It would be a pretty sad story if it ended here, but it didn't. The resurrection got everybody's attention!

"Alive? What do you mean, He's alive? The stone is rolled away? Angels? An empty tomb? The burial shroud left behind? Mary Magdalene saw Him? So did Peter? And the disciples? Even Thomas? Five hundred people at one time?"

Hope rose within them all. The resurrection changed everything. No more doubts. No more embarrassment. He really *was* the Messiah! Even His brothers could see that. First Corinthians 15:7 settles it: "Then he appeared to James." This second-born brother saw Him risen and glorified—and he believed.

*Faith.* The end of the story is amazing, especially considering its beginning. Jesus' brothers became staunch believers after the resurrection. They *all* saw Him. Acts 1:14 says that Mary the mother of Jesus *and His brothers* were present at His ascension into heaven.

The brothers returned to the Upper Room with the other disciples. They were there on the Day of Pentecost when the Holy Spirit came upon them. James eventually became the pastor of the church at Jerusalem. He wrote the Epistle of James. Judas wrote the Epistle of Jude. They were not only believers, but also leaders in the early church.

What changed them from doubters to disciples? What took them from fear to faith? One thing—the resurrection! It convinced His own brothers that He really was the Son of God.

Real faith doesn't come easily. It was a struggle for our Lord's own brothers and sisters, so it shouldn't surprise us when we struggle with faith as well. But if they, His strongest critics, became convinced, so can we.

There are many things about Jesus that appeal to us. Several aspects of His life, ministry, miracles, and messages speak to us. But one thing stands predominant— the resurrection!

If Jesus really rose from the dead, He is no mortal man. His message must be authentic. His claims must be taken seriously. If He is alive today, it does matter what you do with Him. ✳

# 7

# The Friend
# of Sinners

*The next day John saw Jesus coming toward Him and said, "Look, the Lamb of God, who takes away the sin of the world!"*

John 1:29

John the Baptist created quite a commotion with his preaching in the Judean wilderness. There, along the banks of the Jordan River, he attracted enormous crowds. People poured out of the surrounding cities to hear his dramatic call to repentance.

"Repent, for the kingdom of heaven is near," John thundered (Matthew 3:1).

He was the fulfillment of Isaiah's prophecy (40:3) about a voice calling in the desert (40:3). His whole purpose was to call Israel to repent and prepare for the coming of her King.

"Who are you?" his listeners demanded. "Are you the Messiah? Are you Elijah? Are you *the Prophet* Moses said would come?" "No! No! No!" "Then, who are you?" "A voice crying in the wilderness," was his only response.

Dissatisfied with John's replies, the crowds could only wait and watch as he continued to call people to repentance. Then, one day, John looked up and saw Jesus coming toward him.

Instantly, John blurted out those awesome words: *"Look, the Lamb of God, who takes away the sin of the world!"*

Every first-century Jew understood the significance of a sacrificial lamb. Alfred Edersheim writes, "At the very threshold of the Mosaic dispensation stands the sacrifice of the Paschal Lamb connected with the redemption of Israel."[7]

The Bible affirms this when it states, "Without the shedding of blood there is no forgiveness" (Hebrews 9:22).

*Blood atonement* by a sacrificial lamb was essential to the Old Covenant. In fact, it was called the "blood of the covenant" (Hebrews 9:20). But as the years passed, the time came to institute a New Covenant. This is what Jesus meant when He later gathered His disciples for the Last Supper. "This cup is the new covenant in my blood which is poured out for you," He announced (Luke 22:20).

When John the Baptist made his declaration about Jesus being the Lamb of God, he foresaw the true significance of Jesus: He had come to earth to give His life and blood for the sins of the world. He had come to die!

It may sound like an enigma. But everything in His life was like that.

He was born a King... in a manger.

He was God... in a human body.

His birth was heralded by angels... but His life was nearly snuffed out by Herod's soldiers.

He came to do His Father's business... and that business eventually cost Him His life.

God was in the business of saving sinners. And Jesus went right to them: drunks, harlots, tax collectors, and the like. He never hesitated to reach out to society's rejects.

The self-righteous objected to His compassion. "Why does your teacher eat with tax collectors and 'sinners'?" they demanded of His disciples (Matthew 9:11). Jesus responded, "I have not come to call the righteous, but sinners" (verse 13).

*Sinners* understand Jesus' mission. They appreciate His concern. They need His grace. And they respond to His invitation.

Unfortunately, those of us who have known Christ for a long time often forget what it is like to be a sinner. Oh, we are still sinners, to be sure. We just don't think we are.

Grace, mercy, pardon—those are for *others* who really need such things. We needed them once, too. But that was a long time ago. Now we see ourselves as saints, not sinners. We view ourselves as dispensers of grace rather than objects of grace.

When we arrive at such a state, we lose a *true vision of ourselves.* All too often we forget that we, too, need His grace every day of our lives. We once needed grace to admit we were sinners and to acknowledge our need of a Savior. But we still need His grace to *continue* acknowledging our sins and failures as believers.

Thank God we are not what we were before conversion! But we dare not think that we have arrived at full maturity. There is still a long road ahead for most of us. There is still pride to be dealt with and progress to be made.

*Life is a pilgrimage.* It is a process of growth. There are no shortcuts to maturity; you can only get there by walking the rough road of life. The obstacles, struggles, mistakes, and difficulties along the way remind us we still need the Lamb.

Martin Luther once said, "We are not yet what we shall be but we are growing toward it. The process is not yet finished but it is going on. This is not the end, but it is the road."[8]

We are all pilgrims on the road of life. Never content with the temporal, we press on to the eternal. In every failure we see our limitations and His unlimited grace. We are reminded that we are indeed still sinners. Saved? Yes! But still in need of sanctifying grace. Still in need of the ministry of the Lamb of God.

Still in need of Jesus. ✳

# 8

~

# Taking Center Stage

*he bride belongs to the bridegroom. The
friend who attends the bridegroom waits
and listens for him, and is full of joy
when he hears the bridegroom's voice. That joy is
mine, and it is now complete. He must become
greater; I must become less.*

John 3:29-30

It wasn't easy being John the Baptist. From
the very beginning, John knew his ministry was only
temporary. Like a church steeple pointing men to God,
John had come to point men to the Savior. He was the
forerunner of the Messiah, but was not the Messiah
Himself.

John understood his limitations. He didn't think
he was Elijah, though Jesus later said John had come in
the spirit and power of Elijah (Matthew 11:14). John
knew that he had come to call the nation of Israel to
repentance. His ministry was one of preparation, not
completion.

John was Jesus' cousin, the son of Elizabeth and
Zechariah. He was the baby who leaped in his mother's

womb when Mary, carrying the newly conceived Jesus, entered Elizabeth's house (Luke 1:41). He was enthusiastic in Jesus' presence even before either of them were born.

John was six months older than Jesus and he began his ministry before Jesus began His. John was an austere man who lived in the wilderness of Judea. Like the prophet Elijah before him, John dressed in camel's hair, ate off the land, and lived in isolation like a hermit.

The Baptist's sermons were severe, yet he attracted great crowds. He called upon them to repent of their sins and be baptized. From the very beginning of his ministry, John called upon men to be baptized with water. But all the time, he kept predicting someone would come after him who would baptize people with the Holy Spirit.

Jesus applauded John's courage, tenacity, and devotion. "What did you go out to see?" Jesus asked. "A prophet? Yes, I tell you, and more than a prophet" (Matthew 11:9). The Lord then commended John as the greatest prophet of all time and added an unexpected remark: "Yet he who is least in the kingdom of heaven is greater than he" (Matthew 11:11).

What did Jesus mean?

John stood at the end of a long line of Old Testament prophets. He was the last and greatest of a vanishing breed. But as great as he was, John lived and died before the crucifixion and resurrection of Christ. He was the "friend" of the bridegroom at the Marriage Supper of the Lamb, but neither the bridegroom nor the bride.

John the Baptist marked the transition point between the old and new dispensations. He was the best of the old, but he was less than the least of the new. The lowest saint in the church era who has been baptized by the Holy Spirit into the body of Christ is greater than John.

Certainly Old Testament believers are part of the family of God. But they do not enjoy the same status as the New Testament church. Ours is a unique relationship, just as Old Testament Israel had a unique relationship to God.

John understood this. The time had come for dramatic change. Soon his own disciples were leaving him to follow Jesus and the crowds began to throng after the Savior. No matter to John.

Using the analogy of an ancient wedding, John explained that he was merely the "friend who attends the bridegroom" (John 3:29). We would call him the "best man" in today's weddings. "I'm not the bride [church] or the Bridegroom [Christ]," he explained. Therefore, he could humbly conclude, "He must become greater; I must become less" (John 3:30).

We cannot read this account of John's humility and Jesus' preeminence without asking ourselves, "Am I willing to become less that He might be magnified in my life? Am I willing to surrender my individual priorities that He might become *the* priority in my life?"

When there is too much of me, people see too little of Him. If we are to be successful disciples, we must magnify the Savior and give Him center stage in our lives.

John the Baptist's humility is overwhelming. He willingly steps aside as Jesus takes center stage. From this point on, our Lord is the preeminent person in the Gospel story. All the others pale into insignificance.

Jesus upstages them all—rulers, nobles, scribes, rabbis, soldiers, disciples, saints, and sinners. None compare to Him! Caesar, Herod, Caiaphas, Pilate,

Sadducees, Pharisees, Herodians, and Zealots. None are His equal!

Most of those who appear in the stories of Jesus would have been forgotten long ago were it not for *Him*. Their names would have disappeared from the annals of time. Their monuments have crumbled. Their empires have fallen. Their accomplishments have perished.

But Jesus alone stands towering over the wrecks of time. He is the central figure of history, the greatest man who ever lived. Everyone else in the Gospel record has significance only because their lives touched His life. Their record is left behind only because it is part of *His* record.

There is no greater Savior than Jesus because there is no greater Person than Jesus. The power of His Person, the magnitude of His mission, and the dramatic manner in which He defines human history . . . these set Him apart. There is no one else like Him in all the world. There never has been and there never shall be. He stands alone, above all others.

And He always will. ✳

# 9
~

# The Battle Begins

*esus was led by the Spirit into the desert to be tempted by the devil.*

Matthew 4:1

Jesus . . . tempted? Hold on a minute!

How could the sinless Son of God be tempted to sin? What's more, why would the Holy Spirit *lead* Him into the desert to be tempted in the first place?

The story of Christ's temptation is one of the most powerful accounts in the Gospels (*see* Matthew 4:1-11; Mark 1:12-13; Luke 4:1-13). It is also rife with some tough theological questions.

If Christ is God, and God cannot sin, then wasn't the temptation a farce? Satan didn't stand a chance! How can the Gospel writers call this a *temptation?*

On the other hand, if the temptation were real, how can we say that Christ is sinless? If we use the argument that He *could* have sinned but chose not to sin, are we not suggesting that God *could* sin? And if God could sin, are we not left with a God who is less than sinlessly perfect?

And then the questions really start flowing! Can God sin if He *wants* to sin? Or is His holy nature such that He *cannot* sin? If God *could* sin, am I not left with the fear that He *might* yet commit sin? But if He *cannot* sin, how could Jesus be tempted?

Now you understand what keeps theologians in business! We could continue asking such questions endlessly. But let's stop to consider two basic facts:

1. *God is holy.* The Bible clearly presents God as sinlessly perfect. The prophets called Him the "Holy One." His dwelling place was called the "Holy of Holies." His laws demanded holiness of human character and behavior in conformity to God's holy character and behavior. The Bible views God as absolutely holy in His being and His will; the one is the expression of the other. God is holy and cannot sin because it is not in His nature to sin.

2. *Jesus was tempted.* The Bible emphatically describes our Lord's encounter with Satan as a temptation. In His humanity, Jesus was tempted to the same selfish desires as are we all. He had fasted for 40 days in the barren Judean wilderness. Anyone who has ever visited this area is immediately struck by the lack of vegetation—no trees, no bushes, no food. As a fully human being, Jesus was hungry and tired. He was physically vulnerable to temptation. There is no doubt in the Gospel writers' minds that Christ's temptation was real.

The Bible itself resolves this apparent dilemma. The book of Hebrews explains it this way: "For we do not have a high priest who is unable to sympathize with our weaknesses, but we have one who has been tempted in every way, just as we are—yet was without sin" (4:15).

Jesus is a sympathetic Savior. He understands our struggles with temptation because He too was tempted.

But whereas we are sinful and finite beings, He is a sinless and infinite being. Whereas we are vulnerable to temptation, He is invulnerable to temptation.

Did Satan tempt Jesus? Sure he did! Was the temptation real? Certainly it was! Could Satan have defeated Christ? Of course not!

Theologian W.G.T. Shedd writes, "It is objected . . . [that] a person who cannot sin . . . cannot be tempted to sin. This is not correct; any more than it would be correct to say that because an army cannot be conquered, it cannot be attacked."9

Satan did his very best to bring Jesus down. But Satan's tempting Jesus was like a canoe attacking a battleship. The attack was real, but the outcome was never in doubt. As the "second Adam," Jesus resisted temptation and defeated the tempter.

Satan's attack was clever, well-timed, and insidiously targeted. "If you are the Son of God" he said, "tell these stones to become bread" (Matthew 4:3). First, he implied that Jesus' deity was in some doubt. He was taunting Him to prove it by an act of *self-provision*. But Jesus resisted. In the future, He would have to resist this temptation again. He would have to deny Himself in order to accept our punishment on the cross.

Having failed at the first temptation, Satan tried a second. Again, he raised the question, "If you are the Son of God. . . ." This time, he took the Lord to the pinnacle of the Temple. "Throw yourself down," Satan insisted (verse 6). It was a temptation to *self-protection*. "The angels will catch you," he gleefully suggested. Again, Jesus resisted. This was no time to tempt God the Father with a premature act of self-will. Resistance now would prepare Him to say at Gethsemane, "Not My will, but Yours be done."

Finally, Satan got to the heart of the matter. No more insinuations about not being the Son of God. Satan showed Jesus the kingdoms of the world and promised to surrender them if Christ would worship him. It was a temptation to *self-promotion*. "All this will I give You," Satan promised (verse 9). Here was a shortcut to the Kingdom. No struggle. No rejection. No crucifixion. Just capitulation, compromise . . . and defeat.

"Away from me, Satan!" Jesus bellowed (verse 10), and the Scripture says Satan left Him. Finally, the temptation was over. The Holy Spirit had led Him to the battlefield that He might emerge victorious on our behalf.

As you face the battles of life, you also will face many temptations. There will be temptations to take care of yourself. You will be tempted to cut corners on your responsibilities, to pocket a little extra for yourself, to do whatever it takes to get ahead or to get to the top.

Ask yourself, "What would Jesus do if He were in my place?" Would He sacrifice someone else's career to protect or promote His own? Would He run ahead to get in the front of the line? Would He sacrifice His own ethics and principles in order to close a deal?

We don't have to give in to temptation. Jesus has already won the battle for us. Jesus Christ is more able to deliver us from temptation than we are willing to be delivered. Romans 8:37 says, "In all these things we are more than conquerors through him who loved us."

With victory thus assured, we can face the enemy with confidence—not in ourselves, but in Him. He faced the greatest temptations in history and whipped them decisively. How could it be otherwise? The greatest Savior in history will always conquer the greatest temptations in history.

Every time. ✳

# 10

## Putting Out the Unwelcome Mat

*esus returned to Galilee in the power of the Spirit, and news about him spread through the whole countryside. He taught in their synagogues, and everyone praised him.*

Luke 4:14-15

Popularity is a transitory thing; it comes and it goes. One day you are a hero and the next day you're being fitted with tar and chicken feathers.

It was no different for Jesus. His initial success in Galilee was astonishing. Large crowds were following Him from place to place as He healed the multitudes. People hung on His every word.

But then He went home to Nazareth and it was a different story. At first the townspeople were impressed. They were "amazed at [His] gracious words," the Bible says (Luke 4:22).

"Isn't this Joseph's son?" they asked.

"Why, of course—it's the carpenter's boy," some of the older ones may have responded.

The carpenter had come home. But when He read the Scripture in *their* synagogue and preached to the heart of *their* problems, they became infuriated with Him and tried to throw Him out of town. They even tried to kill Him, but He escaped.

It's a funny thing about preaching. As long as the preacher is talking about someone else's sins, we applaud him. But as soon as he tries to deal with our sins, we get mad.

*What a hypocrite! Who does he think he is? His success has gone to his head! We had better get rid of him for his own good! He's so full of pride, he can't see straight. He should stick to preaching. But now he's gone to meddling!*

We have all heard people talk like that. We may have talked that way a few times ourselves. But it is ugly talk. It is motivated by pride and filled with selfishness, defensiveness, and arrogance.

Jesus' own neighbors threw Him out of town. They wanted to share in His success but they did not want to accept His call to repentance. He called for too much sacrifice.

He could have been more accommodating. He could have complimented them on what a fine town they had. He could have talked "carpenter talk" with them. Boards. Nails. Framing. Roofing. He could have done a few small miracles.

But not Jesus! He told them right up front that He would not put on a show for them. No special effects for the hometown crowd. No miracles that they could gloat over. Just straightforward preaching... and they didn't want to hear it.

"He... went on His way," the Bible simply says (Luke 4:30). When the people of Nazareth refused to listen, Jesus stopped talking and went to Capernaum.

There, His message found great acceptance. Luke 4:32 states, "They were amazed at his teaching, because his message had authority."

Things were different in Capernaum. They put no demands on Him. There were no requests for special favors. He healed the sick and preached with power and authority. "And the news about him spread throughout the surrounding area" (Luke 4:37).

Jesus did not come to be popular. He came to tell us the truth about God and about ourselves. It is easy for us to think we would have accepted Him. Surely we would not react like those ungrateful people from Nazareth!

*But are we really listening?* How many times have we refused to listen when Jesus spoke to us? As we search the Scriptures, we hear His voice so many times telling *us* things we would rather not hear:

- "If someone strikes you on the right cheek, turn to him the other also" (Matthew 5:39).

- "Love your enemies and pray for those who persecute you" (Matthew 5:44).

- "First go and be reconciled to your brother; then come and offer your gift" (Matthew 5:24).

- "If you do not forgive men their sins, your Father will not forgive your sins" (Matthew 6:15).

- "Not everyone who says to me, 'Lord, Lord,' will enter the kingdom of heaven" (Matthew 7:21).

When Jesus calls today, will you hear Him? Will you heed His call? Will you obey His request? Or will you be so busy telling Him what to do for you that you can't hear Him at all?

"Lord, bless me! Do this and that for me! Give me a happy life! Take away all my pressures and problems!"

Sacrifice? You've got to be kidding!

Surrender? But it's my life!

Service? That's for others! I've done my bit!

Jesus may have *looked* like a carpenter, but He was much more than a carpenter. He was God. And when God talks, it's time to listen. We may not always like what He has to say, but the fact that He says it makes it significant.

Nazareth would never again know the joy of Jesus' presence. His ministry would take Him elsewhere . . . Capernaum, Bethsaida, Caesarea Philippi, Bethany, Jericho, Jerusalem. But He never returned to Nazareth.

God had spoken. The people had refused His message. And God moved on.

You need to ask yourself: Am I listening when God is speaking? Or am I missing the message He has for me?

Go back and read our text again in light of your own response to Christ. Are you willing to listen only when He tells you what you *want* to hear, or are you willing to listen to what you *need* to hear?

Are you willing to follow the Savior's call? ✳

# 11

## Fishers of Men

*C*ome, follow me," Jesus said, "and I will
make you fishers of men." At once they left
their nets and followed him.

Matthew 4:19-20

Fishing was a good business in Galilee. The
large, freshwater lake supported many fishermen. They
were simple people, men of habit. Predictable.
Dependable. Most were devout Jews. Sincere. Family
men. Men who did not easily change their way of life.

They had met Jesus before. John the Baptist had
introduced Him to Andrew, James, and John. Andrew
told his brother Peter that he was convinced Jesus was
the Messiah (John 1:41). Next, Jesus called Philip, and
Philip told Nathanael, "We have found the one Moses
wrote about" (John 1:45). But when Nathanael heard
Jesus was from Nazareth, he was shocked.

"Nazareth! Can any good thing come from
there?"

Yet there was something impressive about Jesus.
He was not the typical self-righteous, radical religious
leader. There were no delusions of grandeur. In fact, He

often cautioned His followers not to tell people He was the Messiah.

There was a genuine humility about Jesus. He was a blend of gentleness and strength, wisdom and practicality. But more than anything else, He was the epitome of spiritual authority. Each of His disciples was profoundly impressed by their first encounter with the 30-year-old Teacher.

Some time had passed now since those first meetings. Jesus was walking along the shore of the Sea of Galilee and spotted Peter and Andrew in their boats. "Come follow Me," He said.

His call was dramatic. Not demanding nor degrading, but irresistible. Even tantalizing.

"I will make you fishers of men," He explained.

Immediately, they left their boats and followed Him. So did James and John. They had considered His claims long enough. Now it was time to act. The moment of decision had come.

Jesus was calling them to a greater degree of commitment than they had ever known. He wasn't merely asking them to believe in Him. He was asking them to act upon their beliefs.

"If I am really who you say I am," He may have said, "then do something about it!"

It wasn't easy leaving their business behind. It was their livelihood and their life. It was all they had ever known.

But Jesus' call was clear, His invitation irresistible. And the task before them was greater than any they had ever imagined. They were no longer to fish for food for the table; now they were to fish for men for the kingdom.

What a challenge! What a privilege! John Pollock writes, "To the numerous travelers who passed them, they seemed a small party of disciples with their rabbi, a sight almost as common as a camel caravan or a posse of soldiers."[10]

But they knew who they were. They were ambassadors of the King of kings. They were about the Father's business. They were on an adventure to serve the King. They were fishing for men. They were engaged in royal service. They were standing arm-in-arm with the Messiah. They were about to bring in the kingdom.

Or, so they thought.

*Discipleship is no easy task.* In time, these fishermen would learn what true discipleship was really all about. Even after three years of following Jesus they would be filled with questions, doubts, and fears—even to the very end.

They were learning what it meant to be disciples. Indeed, to be Christians. To be like Christ. Yet, so often they would fall short. The Savior would have to rebuke their selfishness, their unsubmissiveness, their lack of faith.

They had a lot of growing to do. But they had set out on the greatest adventure of life. They would see the Savior heal the sick, give sight to the blind, raise the dead, walk on water, and feed the multitudes.

They would personally witness His miracles. And they would personally hear His messages—sermons so profound that they are still the greatest thoughts ever expressed. The depths of truth and goodness in His words have never been exhausted. The power of His messages still confronts us today and demands that we, too, forsake all and follow Him.

Charles Spurgeon said, "To come to Jesus not only implies leaving all other confidences, and trusting

Christ, it also means following Him. If you *trust* Him, you must *obey* Him."[11]

Discipleship results in obedience. Only as the disciples learned to obey Christ's teaching did they become effective at fishing for men. Oh, they had a few successes, to be sure. But their failures far outnumbered them. "Your disciples could not . . ." were the condemning words they often heard from those disappointed by their efforts.

Anybody can get excited about going fishing. You obtain a license, buy the tackle, get your bait and lures. But *doing* the fishing is another matter. It takes time, discipline, and patience. It also takes determination. You have to go where the fish are if you are going to catch any.

As you go about your life today, ask yourself: Am I going fishing, or am I just paddling around in the pond? Am I committed to obeying Christ, or am I looking out for my own interests? Is Jesus' business really my business, or am I too busy to follow Him?

True discipleship means forsaking all to follow the Savior. ✳

# 12
~

# It Costs to Follow Jesus

*fter this, Jesus went out and saw a tax collector by the name of Levi sitting at his tax booth. "Follow me," Jesus said to him, and Levi got up, left everything and followed him.*

Luke 5:27-28

Jesus made no apologies when He called His disciples. He was direct and decisive. He didn't beg or plead. He made no promises of blessing or comfort. "Follow Me," is all He said.

And people dropped everything to follow Him.

We cannot read the Gospel accounts of our Lord calling His disciples without being impressed by their immediate response.

Fishermen already had dropped their nets to follow Him; now a wealthy tax collector leaves his money on the table at the customs counter and follows the Savior.

Most of us know Levi by the name of Matthew. He later wrote one of the Gospels. Levi is the name of the family of priests. The book of Leviticus takes its name from this tribe of Israelites who held a special place of prominence among the Jews.

Matthew, however, had fallen from grace among his Jewish relatives. He had sunk about as low as a backslidden Jew could go. This Levite had become a *tax collector!* A publican! A collaborator with pagan Rome! How disgusting!

But Jesus was in the business of saving sinners, reclaiming backsliders, transforming lives. No one was so low as to be beyond the touch of His grace.

We can only assume from Matthew's numerous quotations of the Old Testament that he had an extensive knowledge of the Hebrew Scriptures. Perhaps he had even trained to be a priest. But somewhere along the line, the lure of money had taken him far away from God.

Now, suddenly and dramatically, he was confronted by the call and claims of Jesus of Nazareth. And without any hint of hesitation, Matthew bolted his old life and followed the Master. Don't think it was an impulsive act! Clearly he had thought about it beforehand. He was not a man to act rashly; he knew what he would be giving up. Yet when the opportunity arose to join Jesus, Matthew jumped at it.

Like Matthew, we too must consider the cost of discipleship. You don't just join up with Jesus like you would join a social club or political organization. Jesus isn't looking for joiners. He is looking for followers. For *real* disciples.

John MacArthur writes, "A Christian is not one who simply buys 'fire insurance,' who signs up just to avoid an unpleasant afterlife. A Christian . . . is one whose faith expresses itself in submission and obedience.

A Christian is one who follows Christ, one who is committed unquestioningly to Christ as Lord and Savior. . . . The call to Christian discipleship explicitly demands just that kind of total dedication. It is full commitment, with nothing knowingly or deliberately held back."[12]

Too many people today call themselves disciples who are not disciples at all. They talk about prayer, but they never pray. They claim to believe the Bible, but they never read it. They acknowledge that eternity is important, but they only live for the present. They call themselves disciples, but they are unwilling to pay the price of discipleship.

Jesus dealt with people like that all the time. And He turned them away! Luke records the incident of a man who said, "I will follow you wherever you go" (Luke 9:57). But Jesus replied, "Foxes have holes and birds of the air have nests, but the Son of Man has no place to lay his head" (verse 58).

Jesus saw past this man's momentary enthusiasm into the depths of his heart. He reminded him that there would be sacrifices to be made in following Him. Just as a businessman sacrifices for his business, or an athlete spends untold hours of practice for his sport, or an artist lives in virtual poverty for the sake of his art, so also does Jesus call us to count the cost of following Him.

Yet we must *respond* when we are called. The Gospels tell us of other would-be disciples who would not come when they were called. "Lord, first let me go and bury my father," one said (Luke 9:59). "First let me go back and say good-by to my family," another responded (Luke 9:61).

Perhaps the most striking example is that of the rich young ruler (Luke 18:18-30). He claimed that he wanted to receive eternal life. He also claimed that he had kept the Law. That implied he loved God with all his heart and his neighbor as himself. Any good Jew understood those demands of the Law. But living them was another matter.

To expose the young man's unwillingness to love both God and neighbor more than himself, Jesus said, "Sell everything you have and give to the poor, and you will have treasure in heaven. Then come, follow me" (verse 22).

When the ruler heard the Lord's demands, he grew very sad and turned away. He failed the test of discipleship. He did not respond when Jesus called. And he went away . . . lost.

There is an urgency about following Jesus. And there is a priority in following Him. He takes precedence over all other obligations. When He calls, we must forsake all and follow Him.

Jesus said, "No one who puts his hand to the plow and looks back is fit for service in the kingdom of God" (Luke 9:62). We cannot come to Jesus with double standards. We cannot ask one thing of others and do something less ourselves. We cannot come to Jesus with double allegiance. Either He is Lord or He isn't. Either we forsake all and follow Him or we don't follow Him.

Like Lot's wife, who wanted to linger on the outskirts of Sodom, we put ourselves in jeopardy when we look back and question our decision. If you are going to follow Jesus, then do it. If not, then forget it.

There are no halfhearted disciples in God's kingdom. Peter understood this. So did the Twelve. "We have left all we had to follow you," Peter said (Luke 18:28). Jesus replied by saying that they hadn't left anything that they wouldn't receive many times over in this life and eternal life in the age to come.

What we give up for Christ cannot compare to what we gain in Christ. It is like trading pebbles for diamonds, dirt for gold. It is trading the temporal for the eternal.

And the price of discipleship always yields eternal dividends. ✳

# 13

## Miracles Still Happen

*esus said to the servants, "Fill the jars with water"; so they filled them to the brim. Then he told them, "Now draw some out and take it to the master of the banquet."*

John 2:7-8

It seems most appropriate that Jesus' first public miracle was at a wedding. After all, He had come to call a bride unto Himself. He too would be a Bridegroom, married unto His church.

The little town of Cana lies a couple of miles away from Nazareth. It was a familiar place to Jesus' family. His Mother, Mary, may have been serving as a hostess at the wedding; at least she was concerned about the wine running out. It would be a social embarrassment to run out of wine at the reception or wedding banquet.

"They have no more wine," Mary told her son. The not-so-subtle implication: *Do something. I know You can.*

"Dear woman, why do you involve me?" Jesus replied. "My time has not yet come" (Luke 2:4).

She wanted a miracle. He wanted to wait.

"Do whatever He tells you," she told the servants.

Mary could probably tell by the look on Jesus' face that He would do it for her, if for no one else. In this story we see a glimpse of His mercy and His power. He did care about the newlywed couple's plight. Jesus cares even about the little things in our lives.

The story also tells us why Jesus came to earth. It helps us understand His life and mission. It also helps us remember what we are so quick to forget—that Christ alone is the life of the party.

*He came to fill our emptiness.* Six empty stone water pots sat nearby, used for ceremonial cleansing. "Fill these," He commanded.

Why they were empty we can only guess. An oversight? Already used up? No one knows. But one thing was obvious—they were empty. And filling them was a prerequisite to the miracle that followed.

You too may feel empty and drained right now. You need a special touch from God. Your soul needs to be filled with His presence. Don't try to go on empty! Let God fill your soul again.

*He came to meet our needs.* When the host tasted the water turned to wine, he was overjoyed. He even complimented the bridegroom on its quality. "You have saved the best till now," he said.

The miracle had occurred when they drew out the water from the stone jars. Water went in, but wine came out! There is no indication in this passage that Jesus said or did anything else.

"Fill the jars with water," is all He said. "Now draw some out," He commanded.

What a strange command it must have seemed. Draw water out of the stone jars and take it to the host? *He will think we are mad*, the servants must have thought.

But there was something about Jesus, so they did what He said. And the water miraculously turned to wine.

"The first of his miraculous signs," John called it (2:11). And truly a miracle it was! A miracle over the power of nature itself. That which was one thing became another. That which was inadequate became more than adequate. It prefigured the miraculous transformation that Christ alone can bring to our hearts and lives.

Do you need a miracle in your life today? Jesus is still in the business of meeting our needs. Even if it takes a miracle to do it.

*He came to solve our problems.* We don't know who the bride and bridegroom were. All we know is that they were blessed by the Savior's presence. His power to solve life's problems became evident even at a simple wedding reception.

We can argue about whether the wine was fermented or just grape juice. But what seems most important is that this same substance was later used by our Lord to symbolize His blood that was shed for us on the cross.

Not only was the wine sufficient for the reception, but so also is Jesus' blood sufficient for our sins. He who solved a social problem at a wedding banquet solves our spiritual problems at the Marriage Supper of the Lamb.

The Bible describes our spiritual plight in graphic terms:

*Blind... lost... dead... orphaned... widowed.*

Jesus came to solve every one of those problems!

To the *blind,* He gives sight that they might see and know the truth.

To the *lost,* He is the seeking Shepherd who helps us find our way.

To the spiritually *dead,* He is the very breath of God who breathes life into our souls and gives us eternal life.

To the *orphan,* He is the adoptive Father who adopts us into the family of God and makes us a joint-heir with Himself.

To the *widow,* He is a Bridegroom. He comes to redeem us unto God. He marries us and takes us home to heaven to be with Him.

*He came to resolve our doubts.* The Bible tells us that He revealed His glory through this miracle and that His disciples "put their faith in him" (John 2:11). If they had any doubts about Him before, those were quickly resolved. They had seen His power. There could be no doubt about His Person.

Whenever we let Christ fill our lives with His presence, meet our needs, and solve our problems, He always removes our doubts.

Perhaps you have wandered away from Him. You have felt empty. Maybe you have questioned whether He really cares.

A Savior who cared about a young couple's social embarrassment surely cares about you!

Your deepest needs and your most serious heartaches are exactly what He wants to heal. Don't sit there by the empty water pot of life. Let Jesus fill you to overflowing again.

It's what He does best. ✳

# 14

~

# Are You the One?

*When John heard in prison what Christ was doing, he sent his disciples to ask him, "Are you the one who was to come, or should we expect someone else?"*

Matthew 11:2-3

Prophets have a way of making people angry. They are blunt and sometimes tactless. They don't beat around the bush. They get right to the point.

And that's why they sometimes get themselves tossed behind bars.

Such was John the Baptist's fate. He told King Herod Antipas (Herod the Great's son) that he couldn't lawfully marry his brother's wife, Herodias. So Herod had him arrested and transported to the fortress at Machaerus, in the wilderness east of the Jordan River.

In jail John began to ask himself deep and searching questions. Don't be surprised that he began to question his situation. He probably never expected to end up in jail, let alone face execution.

*Death row!* he may have thought. *I thought we were going to bring in the kingdom! I didn't mind giving up the spotlight—but I didn't mean to exit the stage altogether. We'd better get a few things straight here.*

John wasn't afraid to die; he simply wanted to make sure it was for the right cause. He heard Jesus was preaching in Galilee and attracting great crowds, so he sent messengers to reaffirm that He really was the Messiah.

You may think it a strange request, but when you are facing death, you will probably find yourself asking the same question. Is Jesus really who He said He is? Can I really trust Him with my eternal destiny? Honest questions from people facing life's greatest challenge: death.

Jesus was a prophet Himself, so His reply was to the point: "Go back and report to John what you hear and see: The blind receive sight, the lame walk, those who have leprosy are cured, the deaf hear, the dead are raised, and the good news is preached to the poor" (Matthew 11:4-5).

Here was undeniable proof of His messiahship. Jesus gave sight to the blind. No one had ever done that. There is not one record in the Old Testament of a blind person receiving his sight. Not one!

He raised the dead. Only Elijah and Elisha had ever done that. He was operating on the highest levels of the miraculous. And His greatest miracles were yet to come—the resurrection of Lazarus and Himself!

The lame walked. The deaf heard. Lepers were cleansed. These are miracles performed only by God's greatest miracle-workers. And Jesus did them in abundance!

Yet He was more than a miracle-worker or a healer. He was a preacher of the gospel. "The good news is preached to the poor," he told John's disciples.

The Baptist understood what He meant. It was a fulfillment of Isaiah's prophecy. Isaiah 61:1 predicted of the Messiah, "The Spirit of the Sovereign LORD is on me, because the LORD has anointed me to preach good news to the poor."

Jesus' ministry fulfilled Isaiah's messianic prophecy in Isaiah 35:5-6: "Then will the eyes of the blind be opened and the ears of the deaf unstopped. Then will the lame leap like a deer, and the mute tongue shout for joy."

Our Lord was reminding John the Baptist of all these prophecies he held so dear. Were they being fulfilled? Certainly they were, Jesus replied. It was a message of hope to His cousin, His forerunner, the one who had prepared the way for His ministry.

John "is the Elijah that was to come," Jesus said (Matthew 11:14), referring to the prophecy of Malachi 4:5. He is the "messenger" sent ahead to prepare the way, an allusion to Malachi 3:1.

"There has not risen anyone greater than John the Baptist," Jesus proclaimed (Matthew 11:11). He was the greatest of the prophets. But even *he* wanted to be assured that Jesus was the One.

John found further confirmation in Jesus' superior moral integrity. Jesus towers above everyone in the Gospel accounts. He is more kind, more wise, more gracious than anyone else. His love is abundant. His grace is exuberant. His mercy is endless. He is morally superior in every way.

"To what can I compare this generation?" Jesus asked. "They are like children sitting in the market-places," He explained (Matthew 11:16). They were like immature children, playing while their mothers shopped in the market. To pass the time, they would play their flutes to other children and expect them to respond accordingly. To them, life was a game.

Jesus said, "Wisdom is proved right by her actions" (Matthew 11:19). John the Baptist was a hermit and people thought he had a demon. Jesus was a friend of sinners and they thought He had a demon as well.

You can't study Jesus' life and message and walk away unresponsive. His very nature demands that we make a choice. What's more, His call to discipleship demands that we make a choice. Either Christ or the world. Which will it be?

It's quite a choice! All or nothing. Jesus or the world. This life or the next. Time or eternity. His way or my way.

You, too, may be asking: Is He really the One? Or, do I look for someone else?

The disciples were faced with the same choice when multitudes began turning away from Him. "You do not want to leave too, do you?" He asked the Twelve. But Peter answered, "Lord, to whom shall we go? You have the words of eternal life" (John 6:68).

If Jesus is not the answer, then who is? What other valid options do you have? Dead religions? Deceased leaders? Ritualistic structures? Legalistic regulations? Empty rituals? Mystical experiences?

No, the true and living Savior is the only viable answer. There is none like Him!

When at last we realize what we really want, we see that Jesus is all we really need. ✳

# 15

## Liar, Lunatic, or Lord?

*T*he *Father loves the Son and has placed*
*everything in his hands. Whoever*
*believes in the Son has eternal life, but*
*whoever rejects the Son will not see life, for God's*
*wrath remains on him.*

John 3:35-36

The Bible makes some bold claims about Jesus
Christ. It presents Him as the Son of God, the Savior of
the world, and the Lord of the universe. The New
Testament even goes so far as to insist that our eternal
salvation depends on our faith in Him.

You cannot read very far in the Gospels without
asking yourself some serious questions:

Was Jesus who He claimed to be?
Is He really the only Savior?
Can I trust what He said?
Does it matter what I do with Him?

During the past 2000 years, millions of people have
claimed Him as their Savior. They have staked their

eternal destiny upon His promises. And they have ordered their lives according to His precepts.

If the story of Jesus is a lie, it is the greatest hoax ever perpetrated on the human race. But if it is the truth, then we must take Him seriously. To fail to do so could cost us everything.

Each of us must stop at some point and consider the question: Who is Jesus Christ? Was He a deceiver? Was He deceived? Or was He divine?

The Old Testament was written by numerous authors over a period of 1500 years. Yet, from beginning to end, the Old Testament consistently and congruously predicted the coming of Christ. Consider just a few examples of these predictions:

| | |
|---|---|
| Genesis 22:18 | Born of the seed of Abraham |
| Genesis 49:10 | Born of the Tribe of Judah |
| Jeremiah 23:5 | Born of the house of David |
| Isaiah 7:14 | Born of a virgin |
| Micah 5:2 | Born in the town of Bethlehem |
| Isaiah 9:7 | Heir to the throne of David |
| Isaiah 53:3 | Rejected by His own people |
| Psalm 41:9 | Betrayed by a friend |
| Zechariah 11:12 | Betrayed for 30 pieces of silver |
| Isaiah 53:12 | Executed with criminals |
| Psalm 22:16 | Pierced through the hands and feet |
| Zechariah 12:10 | Crucified (*see* also Zechariah 13:6) |
| Isaiah 53:9 | Buried with the rich |
| Isaiah 53:5 | Atonement for all our sins |
| Psalm 16:10 | Resurrected from the dead |

It is highly unlikely that Jesus could have fulfilled all these prophecies by chance. It is also improbable that He deliberately tried to fulfill them. He had no human control over where and how He would be born, live, and die. All these fulfilled prophecies cannot be mere coincidence. Each one builds upon the others. Add them together and you have convincing proof that Jesus was the predicted Messiah.

Second, you cannot read the New Testament without concluding that Jesus claimed to be God. That claim brought charges of blasphemy, cries of anger, attempts at stoning, and finally, the crucifixion itself.

Why did the religious leaders demand that He be put to death? Because they understood the serious nature of His claims:

John 4:26  "I am he" (the Messiah).
John 5:23  "He who does not honor the Son does not honor the Father."
John 5:39  "These are the Scriptures that testify about me."
John 6:40  "Everyone who looks to the Son and believes in him shall have eternal life, and I will raise him up at the last day."
John 8:58  "Before Abraham was born, I am!"
John 10:30  "I and the Father are one."
John 14:9  "Anyone who has seen me has seen the Father."

Jesus claimed to have come from heaven, to be equal with God, to be the very incarnation of God, and to represent the power and authority of God. There can be no doubt that He believed He was God.

And yet what a man *is* speaks louder than what he *does*. Look at the character of Jesus and you will see a man without sin, who is pure before all men. Even at

His trial, His accusers found nothing with which to accuse Him. He never spoke an untrue word. He never made a promise He could not keep. His personal integrity was above reproach. He was fully human, yet truly divine.

There is no doubt that the people around Him believed He was God. Look at what they said about Him:

> *John the Baptist*—"Look, the Lamb of God, who takes away the sin of the world!" (John 1:29).

> *John the apostle*—"No one has ever seen God, but God the One and Only, who is at the Father's side, has made him known" (John 1:18).

> *Simon Peter*—"You are the Christ, the Son of the living God" (Matthew 16:16).

> *Nathanael*—"Rabbi, you are the Son of God; you are the King of Israel" (John 1:49).

> *The Samaritans*—"We know that this man really is the Savior of the world" (John 4:42).

> *The Jews*—"He was even calling God his own Father, making himself equal with God" (John 5:18).

> *The disciples*—"We believe and know that you are the Holy One of God" (John 6:69).

> *The disciples in the boat*—"Truly you are the Son of God" (Matthew 14:33).

> *Temple guards*—"No one ever spoke the way this man does" (John 7:46).

*Martha*—"Yes, Lord. . . . I believe that you are the Christ, the Son of God" (John 11:27).

*Pontias Pilate*—"I find no fault in him" (John 19:6 KJV).

*Roman centurion*—"Surely he was the Son of God!" (Matthew 27:54).

*Doubting Thomas*—"My Lord and my God!" (John 20:28).

After you evaluate all the evidence for yourself, you too must ask: Who is Jesus Christ? Liar? Lunatic? or Lord?

If He is a *liar* who deliberately deceived others, He is not worthy of your worship. If He is a *lunatic*, self-deceived, and out of touch with reality, He is not worthy of your devotion. But if He is indeed *Lord of lords*, then you have no choice but to bow down and worship Him as your Lord.

C.S. Lewis said, "A man who was merely a man and said the sort of things Jesus said would not be a great moral teacher. He would either be a lunatic—on the level with a man who says he is a poached egg—or else he would be the Devil of Hell. You must make your choice. Either this man was, and is, the Son of God: or else a madman or something worse. You can shut Him up for a fool; you can spit at Him and kill Him as a demon; or you can fall at His feet and call Him Lord and God."[13]

Which choice will you make? ✳

# Part Two

# No One Ever Spoke Like This

———————— ❊ ————————

*No one ever spoke
the way this man does.*
—John 7:46

# 1

## The Happiness Business

*B*lessed are the poor in spirit, for theirs is the kingdom of heaven. Blessed are those who mourn, for they will be comforted. Blessed are the meek, for they will inherit the earth.

Matthew 5:3-5

Are you searching for true and lasting happiness? You can find it in Jesus. He came to conquer our misery and give us His joy.

Our Lord did not come to make people miserable. He came to remove their misery and make them happy. Jesus said, "I have told you this so that my joy may be in you and that your joy may be complete" (John 15:11).

While the Old Testament ended with the threat of a *curse*, the New Testament begins with the promise of *blessing*. "Blessed" (or "happy") are those who live the life that Jesus describes. The word "blessed" comes from the Greek word *makarios*, which means to "be happy." As John MacArthur puts it, "Jesus is in the happiness business."[1]

That is what the Beatitudes in Matthew 5:3-12 are all about. They teach us the "be-happy-attitudes" that make life worth living. Each one comes with both a characteristic and a promise. For example, the poor in spirit receive the kingdom of heaven.

Each description is *spiritual* in nature. Jesus is not merely saying blessed are the poor, the sorrowful, the meek, the hungry—as social conditions. He is describing a spiritual condition that results in a spiritual blessing.

Nor is our Lord merely talking about some future blissful state beyond this life. These are promises of present blessings that can be experienced here and now. Arthur Pink observes, "Christ began not by pronouncing maledictions on the wicked, but benedictions on His people."[2]

Jesus spoke very clearly about those who are truly happy. Let's look at what He said about them.

The *poor in spirit* are the opposite of the proud, the arrogant, the self-righteous. They are, in fact, spiritual "beggars." They have acknowledged their need for God's grace and have accepted His salvation as a free gift. Therefore, they will inherit the kingdom of heaven.

The sorrow of *those who mourn* shall be turned to joy. The agony of their self-condemnation shall cease when they appropriate the comfort of Christ, the lover of their souls. This beatitude is a great enigma to the unsaved: How can those who mourn also rejoice? As incredible as it seems, we can do so because Christ— and not our circumstances—is the real source of our joy. We can live above our circumstances because the Savior lives within us.

The *meek* are those humble souls who dare not trust in themselves, their strength, their power, or their ability. These folks realize their only hope is in Christ, not themselves. Because they trust in *His* ability, power, and strength, they shall inherit the earth. This beatitude is quoted from Psalm 37:11. Only those who have taken on the Christlike quality of meekness are fit to be citizens of His kingdom.

When Jesus speaks of those who *hunger and thirst for righteousness*, there can be no doubt that He is talking about spiritual qualities. Those who are spiritually poor and needy recognize the depth of their condition and hunger and thirst for the righteousness that God alone can give them. They are candidates for grace. They cannot save themselves. They realize their unrighteousness and they cry out to God for the gift of His righteousness. And they shall "be filled"! Theirs will be the complete and total satisfaction of salvation. Psalm 107:9 promises, "He satisfies the thirsty and fills the hungry with good things."

The *merciful* are those who have received mercy. Having been forgiven, they in turn forgive. Jesus describes their attitude when He later urges us, "Love your enemies and pray for those who persecute you" (Matthew 5:44). "If your brother sins, rebuke him, and if he repents, forgive him" (Luke 17:3)—even if he does it seven times or 77 times (Matthew 18:21-22). Those who have been forgiven become forgiving. Those who show mercy will receive mercy.

The *pure in heart* are the only people who will see God. Only those whose hearts have been cleansed by God will see Him. Hebrews 12:14 puts it this way: "Without holiness no one will see the Lord." We cannot approach the throne of God in the defilement of our sin. We must be cleansed and made pure.

83

Revelation 4:2-11 describes the awesome, terrifying, and unapproachable throne of God in heaven, where angelic beings cry: "Holy, holy, holy is the Lord God Almighty" (verse 8). The brilliant radiance of God's glory is there; so are the emerald rainbow, the crystal sea, and flashes of lightning and peals of thunder. No one is worthy to approach that throne except Jesus Christ, the Lamb of God. He alone can make us pure enough to see God because He has purchased us by His blood and cleansed our sins.

The *peacemakers* are God's ambassadors of peace to a fallen world. This is one of the greatest characteristics of citizens of the kingdom. They do not retaliate evil for evil, but rather respond with peace and humility because they trust in God. As such, we should be the problem-solvers and peacemakers in our families, our neighbor-hoods, our churches, and in society itself. Unregenerate society cannot solve its problems without a personal relationship with the Prince of Peace.

Those who stand for righteousness' sake will almost always suffer some form of persecution. They are the persecuted. Do people reject or belittle you for your faith in Christ? Do the unrighteous despise your beliefs and convictions? It is because your life is exposing their evil ways. Notice that, in response, Jesus told us to "rejoice and be glad" (Matthew 5:12). Such persecution demonstrates our faithfulness to Christ. The world has always hated Him. Why should we expect any better?

No one can read these beatitudes without being personally convicted by Jesus' description of true spirituality. We fall short in so many areas. We often feel like giving up altogether.

But wait—read on! Jesus calls us the "salt of the earth" and the "light of the world" (verses 13-16).

Despite our shortcomings, He wants to use us to change the world by letting Him first change us. As we become meek, merciful, righteous, and pure, we are becoming like Christ Himself.

And becoming Christlike is what makes us truly happy. ✳

# 2

## Let's Get Something Straight

*You have heard that it was said, "Eye for eye, and tooth for tooth." But I tell you. Do not resist an evil person. If someone strikes you on the right cheek, turn to him the other also.*

Matthew 5:38-39

Jesus' teaching was so superior to anything anyone had ever heard that people were amazed. He taught them with spiritual authority and personal conviction. He spoke from His heart and people's hearts were moved by what He said.

"Do not think that I have come to abolish the Law or the Prophets," He said, "but to fulfill them" (Matthew 5:17). His purpose was to clarify the true spiritual intention of the Law. Over the centuries Israel's lawkeeping had deteriorated into endless lists of obligations. The people had lost the true significance of the Law.

Jesus set out to remedy the situation. "You have heard that it was said..." He would begin, summarizing the popular misconceptions of Old Testament Law. "But

I tell you . . ." He would insist. In other words, "You think the Law means *this*, but I tell you it means *that*.

This simple formula runs all the way through the Sermon on the Mount (Matthew 5–7).

| *You have heard that it was said* | *But I tell you* |
|---|---|
| 1. Do not murder | 1. Do not be angry |
| 2. Do not commit adultery | 2. Do not lust |
| 3. Divorce requires a legal certificate | 3. Do not divorce except for unfaithfulness |
| 4. Keep your oaths | 4. Do not swear at all |
| 5. Eye for eye; tooth for tooth | 5. Turn the other cheek |
| 6. Love your neighbor | 6. Love your enemies |

The greatness of Jesus' teaching is in its clarity, simplicity, and decisiveness. He cut through all the legal complications and got right to the heart of the matter. He wanted us to see that righteousness—right living—was a matter of the heart. It was not a matter of external compliance, but of internal commitment.

Some have objected that it is impossible to live as Jesus said we should. And by human effort it certainly is! But not through God's power. He alone can enable us to live like Christ—to live like citizens of heaven, not citizens of earth. He alone can empower us to live as if we were in heaven while we are still on earth.

Jesus illustrated real heavenly living. In Matthew 5–7 He gave seven specific examples of how we are to live in such a way as to make a difference in the world.

*By giving.* We are to give quietly unto the Lord. We are not to make a show of our gifts. Calling attention to ourselves is unnecessary. God keeps the books; He balances the accounts. He sees our private devotion and rewards us accordingly.

*By praying.* Likewise, we are not to call attention to our prayers and devotions. Unnecessary public displays steal the focus from the One who is the object of our prayers. God and God alone must have the spotlight. We pray, He answers. We wait, He moves. Ours is the request, His is the response.

*By fasting.* Again, do it privately unto the Lord. Don't make a public show of your self-denial. Don't make it obvious that you are trying to be spiritual. Some people try so hard they turn a simple spiritual discipline into a major platform for self-promotion.

*By possessing.* The blessings of God are so wonderful that we can easily be tempted to focus on *them* and forget about *Him*. We can get so excited about our blessing that we neglect our Blesser. Divided loyalties and split allegiances will not do. It must be either Christ or money. Which will it be?

*By not worrying.* Why do people worry? Because they don't trust! Stop worrying about the things of this life. Start praying about the values of the next life. "Seek first his kingdom" (6:33) and God will take care of your worries. Put Him first and everything else will fall in its proper place.

*By not judging.* It is always easier to judge the motives of others than to get honest with ourselves. Hypocritical self-righteousness always wants to point the finger rather than bend the knee. But Jesus reminds us to take care of the plank in our own eye before trying to remove the speck in someone else's eye.

*By seeking.* Don't sit back, waiting for God to do your job for you. Ask and you will receive. Seek and you will find. Knock and the door will open. If an earthly father will answer his own children when they come calling, how much more will your heavenly Father respond! But we must ask. We must choose the narrow road. And we must pursue Him who has already claimed us as His own. A.W. Tozer has called this the paradox of the burning heart. He writes:

> Come near to the holy men and women of the past and you will soon feel the heat of their desire after God. They mourned for Him, they prayed and wrestled and sought for Him day and night, in season and out, and when they found Him the finding was all the sweeter for the long seeking.[3] ✳

# 3

~

# He Spoke in Parables

*T*hen he told them many things in *parables, saying: A farmer went out to sow his seed. . . . He who has ears, let him hear.*

Matthew 13:3,9

Parables are earthly stories with heavenly meanings, pithy illustrations of profound truths, word pictures to convict the conscience and illuminate the soul. Jesus used them throughout His teaching ministry and without a doubt was the greatest teacher of parables in history.

He used parables not only to clarify issues, but also to separate His listeners. He told His disciples that He spoke in parables to *them* that they might understand, but He spoke in parables to *unbelievers* that they might not understand (Matthew 13:11). "Though seeing, they do not see; though hearing, they do not hear or understand," He said, quoting Isaiah 6:9-10.

But to all believers, He promised, "The knowledge of the secrets of the kingdom of heaven has been given to you" (Matthew 13:11). Parables reveal truth to believers. They provide natural illustrations of supernatural truths.

G. Campbell Morgan writes,

> The parables constituted a lamp . . . that the hidden things might be brought to light. . . . He gave them parabolic pictures, so that they might inquire. The purpose of the story, the picture, was to lure them to think that they might discover deeper truths.[4]

What do you think of when you read the parables of Jesus? Do the illustrations enlighten your understanding? Do they help make the truths more real, the applications more practical?

Look at the Parable of the Sower in Matthew 13:3-8. Jesus used a familiar agricultural illustration of a person sowing seed. The seeds fell from his hand into four types of soil: 1) a path, 2) rocky places, 3) among thorns, and 4) good soil. In each case the response of the seeds was determined by the condition of the soil.

Much has been written on this parable. But its basic meaning was explained by the Lord Himself in Matthew 13:18-23. In those verses Jesus explains that the seed is the gospel ("message about the kingdom"). Satan ("the evil one") snatches away the seed. The types of soil are the types of people who hear the Word and respond to it in various ways.

*Type of Soil:* Path
*Condition:* Hard
*People Illustrated:* Hardhearted
*Response:* None

| | |
|---|---|
| *Type of Soil:* | Rocky Places |
| *Condition:* | Shallow |
| *People Illustrated:* | Shallow |
| *Response:* | Emotional |

| | |
|---|---|
| *Type of Soil:* | Among Thorns |
| *Condition:* | Weeds |
| *People Illustrated:* | Worldy |
| *Response:* | Temporary |

| | |
|---|---|
| *Type of Soil:* | Good Soil |
| *Condition:* | Well plowed |
| *People Illustrated:* | Receptive |
| *Response:* | Genuine |

Notice how Jesus takes the very common experience of farming and uses it to illustrate how people respond to the gospel.

*Hardhearted* people make no response whatever. They are oblivious to the message. You can pour your heart out and they just sit there looking at you with a blank stare. Jesus said they are like seeds sown on the path or roadside. The ground is hard and packed down. The seeds cannot enter the soil and the birds devour them. How did this soil get so hard? From people walking on it. Be careful who or what you let walk on your heart. The harder your heart becomes, the less receptive it is to God's truth.

*Rocky places.* Here Jesus has in mind the rocky ground where it is virtually impossible to grow a crop. The soil is shallow, the plants cannot develop roots, and therefore they soon wither and die. Now, Jesus isn't talking about people losing their salvation; He is illustrating those who make an outward emotional response to the gospel. They receive the message with great joy, but their lives are never transformed by it. They may laugh or cry, but they really do not believe.

*Thorns* represent the worries and cares of this life. These people make a profession of faith but it is neither real nor lasting. The concerns of wealth and prosperity choke out any real response to the gospel. Jesus called it the "deceitfulness of wealth." These people are too concerned about the present to focus on the future. They are so worried about the temporal they can't value the eternal. Theirs is a self-imposed preoccupation with things and it keeps them from the One who could make all the difference.

*Good soil* describes that which has been weeded, tilled, and prepared. It is ready to receive the seed and produce fruit. Jesus said this kind of person "hears the word and understands it." Notice that he not only listens to the message but also grasps its truth. This person produces lasting fruit because he internalizes that truth and it changes his life. Now, fruitfulness may vary depending on the person. Some people produce 100 times, others produce 60 times, and still others produce 30 times what was sown—but they all produce something.

Jesus gave no one the option of producing *no* fruit. To Him, no fruit meant no life. No response equals no reception, which equals no change.

It is obvious that our Lord considered the first three responses inadequate. Only the person whose heart is prepared by the Holy Spirit and truly believes the gospel message will be changed. And only the person who is truly converted will produce evidence (fruit) of that conversion. The amount may vary from one believer to another, but every true believer will show some evidence of spiritual life. Fruit is the evidence of faith.

John MacArthur, Jr. has said:

> Those who teach that obedience and submission are extraneous to saving faith are forced to make a firm but unbiblical distinction between salvation and discipleship. . . . I am convinced that the popularized gospel of the twentieth-century church has made all this possible, even inevitable. The notion that faith is nothing more than believing a few biblical facts caters to human depravity. If repentance, holiness of life, and submission to the lordship of Christ are all optional, why should we expect the redeemed to differ from the heathen?"[5]

There is an essential difference between wheat and weeds. They are not the same. One produces grain (fruit) and the other does not. One represents the true believer, the other does not.

Different soils produce different results. Hard, rocky, thorny soil produces no lasting fruit. Good ground, well-plowed, will always produce fruit—some 100 times, some 60 times, some 30 times—but always something.

Ask yourself: Which am I? Is my life spiritually fruitful? Or is it just a garden of weeds? Who am I, really? What am I? And what am I going to do about it?

Remember, God's Word can only take root in a broken heart. ✳

# 4

~

# Are There Weeds
# in Your Garden?

*esus told them another parable: "The kingdom of heaven is like a man who sowed good seed in his field. But while everyone was sleeping, his enemy came and sowed weeds among the wheat, and went away.*

Matthew 13:24-25

Weeds! Unsightly. Aggravating. Miserable counterfeits. Always popping up where you don't want them. They invade the well-planned gardens of life and disrupt everything in their path.

Jesus used the Parable of the Weeds to illustrate a powerful truth. There are always fakes among the real, counterfeits among the genuine. They look like the real thing but they aren't. They blend in at first, but eventually they stick out because they don't really belong.

Agricultural experts tell us that darnel weeds were a common problem in the wheat fields in Israel. Darnel looks like wheat and it grows like wheat, so it is difficult to detect. The only difference is that darnel produces no wheat. It is worthless.

Have you ever wondered about certain people who claimed to be Christians? At first, they said all the right things. But as time passed, there was little or no spiritual reality in their lives—no spiritual growth, no heart for God, no evidence of lasting change.

Jesus used this parable to remind us that there will always be weeds (those who falsely profess to have faith) among the wheat (true believers). In Matthew 13:24-30 He tells the story and in 13:36-43 He interprets it for us.

"Explain to us the parable of the weeds in the field," the disciples asked. Jesus answered by identifying each symbol in the story:

> The sower is the Son of Man.
>
> The field is the world.
>
> Good seeds are sons of the kingdom.
>
> Weeds are sons of the devil.
>
> The enemy is the devil.
>
> The harvest is the end of the age.
>
> The harvesters are the angels.

With these identities established, we can then interpret the story. Jesus sends us forth to proclaim His gospel and make converts ("sons of the Kingdom"). As the number of converts (the church) grows, they come to fill the world. But in the meantime, Satan sows some false believers among the true to dilute the power of the church and slow its growth.

The issue, then, is this: What shall we do with the weeds? Pluck them up or let them grow? Jesus commands us to let them grow among the wheat until the time of harvest. Then, at the end, God will separate the wheat from the weeds.

Why not pull up the weeds now? Because of the danger of pulling up some of the good grain and damaging the harvest. Later, God's angels will separate the false from the true and cast the weeds into the "fiery furnace" (hell).

There is great wisdom in this parable. It reminds us there will always be false professors. They claim to believe in Jesus Christ but their lives do not bear out their profession. They say they have faith but they have no fruit. They claim one thing but live another. The Lord of the harvest tells us to wait until God sorts it all out at the end.

Some believers think God has called them to pull weeds. They are constantly criticizing and evaluating the lives of others. They have become self-appointed spiritual fruit inspectors. But God never called us to be fruit inspectors; He called us to be fruit *producers*.

In this parable, Jesus also reminds us there will always be weeds among the wheat. We must be wise enough to know the difference. We must also be persistent in distinguishing between that which is true and that which is false. This is a never-ending job. We must do it again and again.

Last, our Lord uses this parable to remind us that He knew what He was doing. We see someone fail or falter and we think, *God, why don't you deal with him?* We want lightning to strike, planes to crash, cars to wreck. But God rarely takes such drastic measures. Sometimes He even extends more grace to people than we think He ought to. We want judgment and He wants mercy.

We cannot always know the mind of God. There will be times when He does things His own way, not ours. We will think He is making a mistake until hindsight tells us otherwise. God's ways are not always our ways, and God's timing is not always our timing. He operates His own clock on an eternal standard.

The real issue is not what time *my* clock indicates, but what time it is on *His* clock. As our wise, sovereign Father, He knows the end from the beginning. There are no surprises on God's timetable.

It's easy to look for weeds in the church. We say, "Old so-and-so, I bet he's lost." "Mrs. Thingmo. She never really changed." "That kid with all those problems. No way he's saved!" And, "The such-and-such family. Boy, they are a mess. Weeds! They're all a bunch of weeds!"

Are you sure? Should we pluck them up? Throw them out of the church? "Discipline them," we say. "Can't just let people get away with this stuff. Somebody ought to do something."

*Somebody will!* Jesus Himself will take care of the weeds. You and I had better attend to our own growth.

It's better for us to ask ourselves if there are any weeds in our own life. Are there weeds of bad attitudes, gossip, complaints, frustration, anger, guilt, worry? We are so good at "masking" these that we usually overlook them altogether. Unsightly weeds! That's what they are. And we don't even see them.

If your Christianity looks like a garden of weeds, perhaps you ought to reexamine your profession of faith. Have you really repented of your sin and believed the message of the gospel? If you're not sure, make sure.

If you really do know the Savior, perhaps it is time to pull some weeds. It may be time to take stock of your life and decide to make some radical changes. Some things may have to go. Some people may have to go. Let God cultivate your heart and remove the weeds.

You can't expect to grow spiritually until you let God eliminate the weeds in your life. ✳

# 5

## Is Repentance Necessary?

*I tell you, no! But unless you repent, you too will all perish.*

Luke 13:3

Repentance sounds a bit old-fashioned, doesn't it? All that sobbing and crying, hearts full of remorse, and promising to do better next time. We don't see much of that anymore in our churches.

We have become too sophisticated for repentance. Most of us would rather be entertained by a good gospel concert, instructed at a seminar, or challenged by a church-growth conference. But repentance . . . who wants to repent?

Ironically, Jesus' sermons were filled with calls to repentance even when He first began His public ministry. Matthew 4:17 says, "From that time on Jesus began to preach, 'Repent, for the kingdom of heaven is near.'"

Jesus unashamedly called people to repent of their sins and believe the good news of the gospel. To be sure, He calls on us to believe His message. But He does not divorce faith from repentance.

The erroneous idea that repentance is not part of the gospel has weakened the message of today's church and damaged the cause of true evangelism. John MacArthur has observed, "This is certainly no time for weak men, weak messages, and weak ministries. What is needed is moral strength and courage, and uncompromising proclamation of the truth that can set people free."[6]

After His resurrection, our Lord assembled the disciples to give them their final instructions. He explained which prophecies applied to Him and "opened their minds so they could understand the Scriptures" (Luke 24:45). Then He told them that "repentance and forgiveness of sins" should be "preached in his name to all nations" (Luke 24:47).

Look at that verse again. *Repentance* is to be preached to all nations. It is essential to the forgiveness of sins. There can be no doubt about the importance of repentance in Jesus' message. Don't let anyone tell you that repentance was for the Jews only, that it was limited to the Old Testament, or that only believers are to repent, not sinners.

Unfortunately, there are those who say that the message of the gospel is simply "believe." Repentance is a "work," they insist. They reason that since the Bible speaks against a gospel of works, repentance must not be part of the gospel.

Strange logic! That's like suggesting that because the Bible says the Scripture is the Word of God, it couldn't have been written on paper because God doesn't write. Or that because Jesus is God, He could never truly be human; therefore, He didn't have a real body.

There is no way around it. Jesus Himself insisted that repentance be preached to all nations.

We would do well to heed His command. Even if it means rejecting the ideas of well-meaning, popular writers and speakers of our day.

The apostles echoed Jesus' teaching on repentance. Paul said, "God . . . commands all people everywhere to repent" (Acts 17:30). That is about as inclusive as you can get! *All* men, *everywhere*. It doesn't leave anybody out. Walter Chantry writes, "This was no optional note on the apostolic trumpet. It was the melody, the theme of their instructions to sinners."[7]

Late in his ministry, Paul assembled the Ephesian elders and reminded them, "You know that I have not hesitated to preach anything that would be helpful to you but have taught you publicly and from house to house. I have declared to both Jews and Greeks that they must turn to God in repentance and have faith in our Lord Jesus" (Acts 20:20-21).

You can't make it any more clear than that. Paul says he preached repentance and faith publicly and privately to both Jews and Gentiles. Both are essential elements of the gospel. We must repent *and* believe.

If we repent, but do not believe, we have not come to saving faith. On the other hand, if we merely believe without repenting, we have still not come to saving faith. It would be like the prodigal son saying he believed his father would forgive him but he had decided to stay in the pig pen anyway!

*True repentance is essential to salvation.* But true repentance is more than sorrow or contrition. You can cry about your sins and their consequences without repenting of them. True repentance involves a change of mind and heart that inevitably results in a change of behavior.

Repentance is not self-reformation. Nor does it result from self-effort. It is the gift of God to needy sinners who confess their total inability to save themselves.

A. W. Tozer said that believe-only salvation makes Jesus "stand hat-in-hand awaiting our verdict on Him, instead of our kneeling with troubled hearts awaiting His verdict on us."[8]

Ask yourself: Have I ever truly repented? Did I ever come to the point where I came to the end of myself and fell at Jesus' feet and asked Him to change my life?

Some people never make any progress spiritually. They have made a verbal profession of faith, but have never repented of their sin. They keep right on sinning and assume they are on their way to heaven.

But Jesus said, "Not everyone who says to me, 'Lord, Lord,' will enter the kingdom of heaven. . . . I will tell them plainly, 'I never knew you. Away from me, you evildoers!'" (Matthew 7:21,23).

Strong language, isn't it? Such words should make all of us take a second look at *our* profession of faith. Are we truly serious about our relationship to Christ? Do we mean business with Him? Have we allowed Him to break our pride and bring our will into submission to His?

Take a few minutes to reflect on your commitment to Him. Ask yourself: "If Jesus' commitment to me were based on my commitment to Him, where would I be in eternity?" Then ask yourself, "What would I do differently today?"

Repentance and faith go hand in hand. We can't believe without repenting and we can't repent without believing. ✻

# 6

## User-Friendly Christianity

*From this time many of his disciples turned back and no longer followed him. "You do not want to leave too, do you?" Jesus asked the Twelve.*

John 6:66-67

User-friendly Christianity is now widely promoted as the best way to grow a church. Yet Jesus never made an effort to go to any church-growth seminars. He didn't seem worried about attracting crowds. Pity, too. He could have avoided a lot of problems in His ministry.

Consider this incident in John 6:60-71. He had just fed the 5000, then claimed He was "the bread of life." Next, He told people no one could come to Him unless the Father draws him or enables him.

"This is a hard teaching," many of His disciples protested. "Who can accept it?" (verse 60).

"Does this offend you?" Jesus asked. "There are some of you who do not believe" (verses 61,64).

Now that's no way to treat the unchurched. These sincere "seekers" needed a chance to reexamine

His claims in light of their own experience. This was no time to get tough with them. Didn't He want a large following? Think of the impression that would have made on the boys in Jerusalem.

Jesus, however, was completely disinterested in such tactics. In fact, He drove these men away! "Many of his disciples turned back," the Bible says, "and no longer followed him" (verse 66).

Then Jesus had the audacity to ask the Twelve if they wanted to leave as well. Didn't He understand *anything* about attracting and holding crowds?

"Go ahead and leave!" He might as well have said.

But the Twelve knew better. That's why they were the Twelve. And yet even one of them wasn't for real!

"Lord, to whom shall we go?" Peter asked on their behalf. "You have the words of eternal life. We believe and know that you are the Holy One of God" (verses 68-69).

The fact is, Jesus had His own style of church growth. It was based on addition by subtraction, on thinning out the ranks. If you're not sure, leave! He never begged anyone to follow Him. He called. He commanded. He demanded. But He never begged.

If you think you've got a better option, then go ahead and try it. But you won't find anything better or more satisfying than real Christianity. It works because it's genuine. It truly does transform the heart and regenerate the soul. Nothing can compare to it.

Jesus cuts through our excuses. There is no fooling Him. He can see right through you. Don't think you can sneak by with anything. He knew the crowds came back for more bread. They wanted the manna, not the message. Free food, not deep truth.

"Stop grumbling among yourselves," He demanded. "Your forefathers ate the manna in the desert, yet they died" (verse 49). "I am the living bread," He insisted. "If any man eats this bread he will live forever" (verses 50-51).

It all came down to their personal relationship to Him. Many said they believed in Him, but when they finally understood who He was, they turned away. He wouldn't put up with their excuses and was constantly challenging the reality of their faith.

So why should we think He would treat us any differently?

Jesus demanded total allegiance. Read the Gospels thoroughly. What do you find? I'll tell you: Someone who thought He was God! Someone who demanded total allegiance to His lordship and authority! "You call me 'Teacher' and 'Lord,' and rightly so," He said, "for that is what I am" (John 13:13).

Jesus claimed to speak the truth, He demanded that we believe that truth, and He calls us to propagate that truth.

If that's so, then why do we think we have to "soft sell" the gospel? Why do we tend to water it down? "Be less demanding and you'll have more converts." Is that so? Then why didn't Jesus use that approach?

Whatever happened to the idea of contending for the faith (Jude 3)? No doubt someone will always say, "Theology divides; love unites." But is that biblical? Is it what Jesus did?

I don't think so. Remember, it was Jesus who said, "Unless you repent, you too will perish" (Luke 13:3). It was the Master who insisted, "If anyone would come after me, he must deny himself and take up his cross daily and follow me" (Luke 9:23).

J. Gresham Machen wrote, "The gospel may yet break forth to bring light and liberty to mankind. But that will be done by the instrumentality, not of theological pacifists who avoid controversy, but of earnest contenders for the faith."9

When Jesus addressed the crowds who followed Him after the Feeding of the 5000, He did all He could to discourage them from following Him for the wrong reasons. They wanted more manna; He had a message. They wanted more miracles; He insisted they acknowledge Him as their Master.

By the end of the day, most of them had left Him. Too tough! Too demanding! One by one they all left.

Except the Twelve. They had sold out . . . lock, stock, and barrel. They had nowhere else to go. They were in too deep to turn back now. Besides, they were convinced He was the Savior.

Stop and ask yourself: "Why am I following Jesus? Because it's exciting? Because He showers me with blessings? Because my friends share my faith? Because it's the right thing to do?"

Am I following Him because of who He is, or because of what He does? Am I committed to His lordship, or am I just interested in His benefits? Am I sold out to His message, or am I only interested in His miracles?

These are tough questions, yet all of us need to examine our own hearts from time to time. Ask yourself: "Is Jesus the most important person in my life? Am I as committed to Him as He is to me? Am I willing to lay down *everything* for the cause of Christ?" If not, why not? If not now, when?

Jesus Christ is the greatest person who ever lived. He calls you into a personal relationship with Himself. He is waiting to hear from you. Why not call upon Him right now? ✳

# 7

# You Must Be
# Born Again

*esus declared, "I tell you the truth, no one can see the kingdom of God unless he is born again."*

John 3:3

Nicodemus meant no harm in coming to Jesus that night. In fact, as a Pharisee and a member of the ruling council of the Sanhedrin, it was quite a risky step for him. He had come to give Jesus his stamp of approval—a vote of confidence, if you will.

"Rabbi, we know you are a teacher who has come from God. For no one could perform the miraculous signs you are doing if God were not with him," he said (John 3:2).

Nicodemus expected Jesus to be impressed with this compliment. But Jesus wasn't. He thought Jesus would congratulate him for his courage. But Jesus didn't.

Instead, Jesus told Nicodemus that *he* needed God's approval. And God's approval would come only to those who were "born again."

We hear that term used a lot these days. It has even worked its way into a few popular songs. Yet there is just as much confusion about what it means today as there was back then.

Nicodemus missed the point altogether. "How can a man be born when he is old?" the ruler asked. Supposing Jesus to be referring to a second physical birth, he overlooked the possibility of a spiritual birth. Still, Nicodemus was genuinely searching for the truth and he was convinced Jesus could help him find it.

As the Pharisee listened to Jesus' insistence that a man be born again, he expressed three concerns to which Jesus gave three answers.

> *Nicodemus:* "How can a man be born when he is old?"
>
> *Jesus:* "Born of water and the Spirit."
>
> *Nicodemus:* "Surely he cannot enter a second time into his mother's womb to be born!"
>
> *Jesus:* "Flesh gives birth to flesh, but the Spirit gives birth to spirit."
>
> *Nicodemus:* "How can this be?"
>
> *Jesus:* "I tell you the truth."

The term "born again" (Greek, *anothen*) may also be translated "born from above," indicating the supernatural origin of regeneration. It means that a spiritually dead soul is made alive by the Spirit of God. It is a spiritual birth in contrast to a physical birth.

One birth is of the flesh, the other is of the Spirit. In physical birth, the water breaks forth and the baby is born. In spiritual birth, the Spirit breaks forth and a person is spiritually born.

How are we born again? By the transforming power of the Holy Spirit. The Bible pictures us as *dead* in sin.

We not only need a Savior who can forgive our sins, but also One who can transform our lives. Jesus made it clear that He can do both. He is in the business of giving life and changing life. When we trust Him as Lord and Savior, we are not just acknowledging *who* He is, we are also believing in *what* He can do for us.

Jesus alone can give spiritual life by sending His Spirit upon a person. In a moment of spiritual transformation, someone who is spiritually dead can be made alive by the Holy Spirit of God.

When we talk about being "born again" we are referring to that spiritual transformation God has done in our hearts. We are not claiming to be perfect; we know we have a lot of growing to do. But we also know that we are no longer dead. We have been born into the family of God by the power of the Spirit.

Think of it like this: Before Jesus Christ came into your life, you were like a prisoner chained to the wall of your own sin. Condemned. Without hope. Locked in a dark cell. You were like a corpse in a morgue, lifeless and still. No life. Nothing at all. Until Jesus burst in by the power of His Spirit.

Charles Wesley portrayed all that in his famous hymn, "And Can It Be That I Should Gain":[10]

> Long my imprisoned spirit lay
> > Fast bound in sin and nature's night;
> Thine eye diffused a quick'ning ray,
> > I woke, the dungeon flamed with light;
> My chains fell off, My heart was free;
> > I rose, went forth and followed Thee.

In response to Nicodemus's questions, Jesus delivered an entire sermon on the nature and importance of the new birth. To help the Jewish ruler understand how it all works, our Lord referred to the time when Moses lifted up the serpent in the wilderness (Numbers 21).

The children of Israel had rebelled against God. He sent venomous snakes among them and many of them died. When they finally cried out in repentance, God told Moses to make a bronze replica of a snake, put it on a pole, and tell the people to look up at it by faith. Those who did so would be healed and live.

"Just as Moses lifted up the snake in the desert," Jesus explained, "so the Son of Man must be lifted up, that everyone who believes in him may have eternal life" (John 3:14-15). He was talking about being lifted up on the cross.

Then Jesus added those familiar words: "For God so loved the world that he gave his one and only Son, that whoever believes in him shall not perish but have eternal life" (John 3:16).

Jesus could not have made it any more clear. *Faith* is the key to our being born again. *Believing* in Him guarantees our eternal life. *Trusting* His payment for our sins sets us free from sin's penalty. He went to the cross to die that we might live.

In the middle of our Lord's discussion about the new birth stands one imperative: "You must be born again" (John 3:7). It is an inescapable demand that comes from the lips of Jesus Himself. He said it. He insists on it.

There is only one legitimate response. You must ask yourself: "Have I been born again?" If not, you can be born again by faith in Jesus Christ. Believe that His payment for your sin is adequate and that His death alone is enough to satisfy God's demands, set you free, and give you life.

When people come face to face with the Lord's demand for a new spiritual birth, they often turn away with the excuse, "But my religion satisfies me." But that is not the issue.

God isn't asking if your religion satisfies *you*; He is asking whether it satisfies *Him!* And God is satisfied only with the sacrificial death of His Son for your sins. Jesus alone can meet the Father's demand. He alone can be "lifted up" in your place. ✻

# 8
~

# How Many People Are Really Saved?

*hen Jesus went through the towns and villages, teaching as he made his way to Jerusalem. Someone asked him, "Lord, are only a few people going to be saved?"*

Luke 13:22-23

Have you ever wondered how many people are really saved? Sometimes we want to think that everyone who professes to be a Christian is going to make it to heaven. Other times, in our more critical moments, we may wonder if anyone is going to make it!

It is tempting to judge the salvation (or lack thereof) of other people. Especially if they have hurt or wronged us. We simply dismiss them as hypocrites or unbelievers. If they belong to churches or denominations other than our own, we are especially suspicious of their Christianity.

For some people, the question of whether many or few will be saved is a matter of theological debate. But notice how Jesus answered the question in Luke 13:23. He didn't talk about numbers. Instead, He exhorted His listeners to do some serious personal reflection. He used their question to make them search their hearts for the real answers to life.

An interesting fact about Jesus is that He never talked merely for the sake of talking. His words were profound, His thoughts deep, and His compassion compelling. He deeply cared about people, and He still does.

When you truly care about people, you have to tell them the truth. No mincing words, no half-truths, no hidden agendas. Just the truth. Clear and straight-forward.

So, how many people will be saved? The answer is twofold: *Fewer* religious people will be saved than we might expect, but *more* lost people will be saved than we might have imagined.

How is that? Look at Luke 13:24. Jesus said that the door to salvation is narrow. A person does not come into a saving relationship with God through any old approach. You will never hear Jesus say, "Just believe in something" or, "All roads lead to the same place."

He makes it crystal clear that He is the only way to heaven. In John 14:6 He said, "I am the way and the truth and the life. No one comes to the Father except through me." That is a very narrow statement. It excludes all other saviors and all other religions.

But it is also a wide-open invitation to all who will believe!

The narrow door to heaven is closed to self-effort and man's good works. But it is as wide open as the grace of God. Those who try to reach God some other way will miss the door. But all who enter by the door will be saved.

Jesus used this analogy elsewhere. In Matthew 7:13-14 He said, "Enter through the narrow gate. For wide is the gate and broad is the road that leads to destruction, and many enter through it. But small is the gate and narrow the road that leads to life, and only a few find it."

Remember that Jesus said this to people who considered themselves religious. He reminded them that in all their pursuit of religion, they had failed to find the gate to heaven. They were working at being good, but they weren't good enough.

In John 10:7-9 Jesus said, "I tell you the truth, I am the gate for the sheep. . . . whoever enters through me will be saved." On at least three different occasions Jesus clearly said He was the only way to heaven.

Jesus' statements were very negative, for they negated all other methods of salvation. But at the same time His words were very positive. He was saying that He was *the* way to God. He did not simply negate all other ways and leave us with no way; He told us that He is indeed *the* way to God.

Jesus is the door. One cannot read the Gospels without concluding that Jesus professed to be the Savior. He claimed to be able to forgive our sins, change our lives, and secure our eternal destiny. He made it perfectly clear that He is the only way to God. Therefore, many who think they are saved but are trusting in something or someone other than Him will be rejected at the gate of heaven.

The door to salvation is open. That is the "good news" of the gospel. While a person must enter the door of salvation through Jesus Christ alone, notice that He is an *open* door! He stands with outstretched arms bidding us welcome into His kingdom. And *many* people will come from the corners of the earth and "take their places at the feast in the kingdom of God" (Luke 13:29).

In Jesus' time, Jewish leaders took a dim view of outsiders. Salvation was believed to be for orthodox Jews only. Jesus' words were a shock to their ears. "You yourselves [will be] thrown out," He warned (verse 28). But many outsiders [Gentiles] will come in by the door and be saved (verse 29). There can be no doubt that our Lord foresaw the Gentiles' response to the gospel and that they would come to comprise a great percentage of His bride, the church.

But let's make Jesus' words personal for a moment. Look at your own life and ask yourself, "Have I entered the family of God by the narrow gate of Jesus' love? Have I really accepted His death on the cross as the sufficient payment for my sins? Have I really believed on Him alone to save me?"

That is what it all comes down to—personal faith. No one else can do it for you. You must make this decision for yourself. You must decide if His invitation is for you and then commit yourself wholly to Him.

Some people will go through life and never make this decision. Of them, Jesus said, "There will be weeping there, and gnashing of teeth" (Luke 13:28). Where? At the gate of heaven. Some people will not get in because they tried to get there on their own. But thank God, many others will come in response to the Savior's invitation. What about you?

The door to heaven is wide open to all who will believe. But it is bolted shut to those who will not. ✳

# 9

# What Is Faith?

*Whoever believes in the Son has eternal life, but whoever rejects the Son will not see life, for God's wrath remains on him.*

John 3:36

Faith is believing. It is an act of trust by which we commit ourselves to someone or something. Jesus put it as simply as possible when He said, "Have faith in God" (Mark 11:22). Believe in God. Believe in His Person, His promises, and His power.

Faith is so important that it is mentioned more than 300 times in the Bible. The first reference to believing God is found in Genesis 15:6, where the Scripture says, "Abram believed the LORD, and he credited it to him as righteousness." This passage is so important that it is repeated three times in the New Testament (Romans 4:3; Galatians 3:6; James 2:23).

Another important Old Testament statement about faith is found in Habakkuk 2:4. There we read that "the righteous will live by his faith." This verse is also repeated three times in the New Testament (Romans 1:17; Galatians 3:11; Hebrews 10:38).

God wants us to understand the importance of faith. It is the key that unlocks the door of salvation. Believing in Christ guarantees eternal life, but rejecting Him seals one's eternal doom.

*Faith is not optional.* Either you believe or you don't. Either you trust God enough to love Him and entrust Him with your life, or you don't really believe Him and therefore can't love and trust Him.

Charles Spurgeon put it like this: "There lies at the bottom of all love a belief in the object loved, as to its loveliness, its merit or capacity to make us happy. If I do not believe in a person, I cannot love him. If I cannot trust God, I cannot love Him."[11]

We love God because He first loved us. We trust Him because He first reached out to us. We respond to Him because He initiated contact with us. After Adam and Eve sinned, they ran away from God. But God came *seeking* them. The father of the prodigal son was looking for him, awaiting his return. Faith is believing that God does love me, that He does care, that His arms are outstretched to receive me.

*Saving faith is reliant trust in Jesus Christ.* It means that I believe He is who He claims to be and that He can do what He says He can do. I believe that He really loves me, that He wants to forgive me, that His death on the cross is sufficient payment for my sins.

Trusting Jesus is more than believing He exists. It is more than believing that He lived a good life or that He died on a cross. It means believing that He is the Savior and that there is no greater Savior.

Faith in Christ means that I believe He died for *me.* That He rose again for *me.* That He is in heaven today interceding for *me.* And that He is coming again for *me*. Faith is my personal response to Jesus Christ. When I truly believe in Him, I am personalizing all that He has done for me, all that He offers to me, and all that He will continue to do on my behalf.

The Bible summarizes God's promise like this: "God has given us eternal life, and this life is in his Son. He who has the Son has life; he who does not have the Son of God does not have life" (1 John 5:11-12). This is about as personal as it gets. Either you have Jesus or you don't. Either you have eternal life or you don't. Faith is the key that unlocks the door to heaven.

How does faith begin? By receiving. God has made us an offer. He has offered to forgive our sins. In fact, He has offered to exchange our sin for Christ's righteousness. Believing that offer to be sincere, we respond by receiving the gift God offers—the gift of eternal life!

We receive God's gift like a beggar reaches out for a piece of bread. We take it by faith. We claim it as our very own. When we receive Jesus Christ as our personal Savior, we receive all the benefits He offers: salvation, forgiveness, acceptance, righteousness, and eternal life.

J. Gresham Machen put it this way:

> The reception of that gift is faith: faith means not doing something but receiving something; it means not the earning of a reward but the acceptance of a gift. A man can never be said to obtain a thing for himself if he obtains it by faith. . . . to say that we are saved only by the one in whom our faith is reposed.[12]

Eventually, faith grows into confidence. Once we become convinced God's offer is for us, our faith grows into confidence in all of God's promises. We become more and more convinced that He really means what He has said. It begins with a simple act of reception and grows into confidence that results in obedience.

A.T. Pierson said, "Faith is such confidence in the faithfulness of God, as leads to a reception of his testimony, to such love and trust as becomes a personal bond of union with him."[13]

*Saving* faith should automatically grow into *living* faith. After all, if we can trust Jesus to take us to heaven, why wouldn't we trust Him to help us through the trials of the day? If His salvation is good enough for the future, why isn't it enough for today?

Faith results in obedience. As our confidence in God grows, it becomes easier to obey His will for our lives. Not only are we saved by faith, but we also grow into spiritual maturity by faith. We walk by faith. We live by faith.

The Bible explains living by faith in this way: "The life I live in the body, I live by faith in the Son of God, who loved me and gave himself for me" (Galatians 2:20). We learn to trust Him with our daily lives because we have trusted Him for our eternal destiny.

Once you step out by faith to take Jesus as your Savior, keep on walking by faith. In time, you will gain the confidence to run the race with Him. But you must begin by taking that first step! No more doubts. No more hesitations. No more excuses. It's time to believe Him. Step out by faith. Trust Him today. ✳

# 10

## Is Jesus Lord of Your Life?

*Y*ou call me "Teacher" and "Lord," and
rightly so, for that is what I am.

John 13:13

Jesus was about to go to the cross and die. His disciples were about to betray Him, deny Him, and forsake Him. Yet, He fixed His eyes on them and affirmed His lordship over them.

"That is what I am," He said emphatically.

Jesus is Lord whether we obey Him or not. His lordship is undeniable. It is who He is. His lordship is not dependent on our making Him Lord of our lives. In fact, the Bible never says one word about *making* Jesus Lord of our lives!

"But I've heard preachers say that," you may protest. Perhaps you have. But that doesn't mean they got it from the Bible.

Charles Spurgeon, one of the greatest preachers of all time, said, "If any man would be saved, he must believe that Jesus Christ is both *Lord* and *God*. Again, you must confess that Jesus Christ is Lord, that is Ruler and Master. You must cheerfully become His disciple, follower and servant."[14]

*Lordship is not an option.* Jesus demanded submission to His lordship. He told His disciples it was His rightful title and position and He referred to them as "servants." As such, He expected them to be obedient and follow His example. He even reminded them that "no servant is greater than his master" (John 13:16).

The real question is *not:* Have you made Jesus Lord of your life? The real question is: Have you bowed your heart in submission to His lordship? John MacArthur observes, "Scripture never speaks of anyone 'making' Christ Lord. . . . The biblical mandate for both sinners and saints is not to 'make' Christ Lord, but rather to bow to his lordship."[15]

*Jesus is Lord because He is supreme.* The Bible presents Jesus Christ as God in human flesh. He is deity incarnate. Therefore He is the "firstborn" of the Father. He is first in rank or priority. No one else compares with Him. He is supreme, preeminent, and unique. There is no one else like Him in all the universe.

*He is Lord of creation.* Jesus has existed from all eternity. He is not a creation of God, but is the eternal God Himself. The Bible says, "Through him all things were made; without him nothing was made that has been made" (John 1:3). Also, "by him all things were created: things in heaven and on earth, visible and invisible" (Colossians 1:16). He is the Creator. It is no wonder He could heal the sick, give sight to the blind, make the lame walk, raise the dead, and still the storms. He has power over His creation because He is the Lord of creation.

*He is Lord of the church.* The church did not invent Jesus Christ; He invented the church. The Bible says,

"He is the head of the body, the church; he is the beginning and the firstborn from among the dead, so that in everything he might have the supremacy" (Colossians 1:18). He is supreme in His resurrection. He is the first person to rise from the dead who shall never die. Therefore, He can say, "I am the resurrection and the life. He who believes in me will live, even though he dies; and whoever lives and believes in me will never die" (John 11:25-26).

*He is Lord of conversion.* When people become saved, we speak of them as having been converted to Christ. The Bible tells us that God reconciles us to Himself "through his blood, shed on the cross" for our sins (Colossians 1:20). Therefore, we are no longer enemies of God. We have been reconciled. The enmity between us has been removed and we are at peace with God because Jesus died in our place. God now views us as "holy . . . without blemish and free from accusation" (Colossians 1:22).

There can be no question about who Jesus is. The Bible makes it clear. The apostles made it clear. And Jesus Himself makes it clear. He is Lord!

The only real question that remains, then, is this: *Is He Lord of your life?* Think through your answer. Remember, lordship implies ownership. Does He own your tongue and what it says? Does He own your eyes and what they see? Does He own your hands and what they touch?

You don't have to be perfect to have Him as your Lord. The disciples to whom He said, "You call me . . . 'Lord' and rightly so" (John 13:13) were far from perfect. In fact, they would deny and forsake Him the very next day!

Jesus' lordship is not conditioned upon our obedience. He is still Lord even when we fail Him. We can sin *against* His lordship, but we can't sin *away* His lordship. Once we belong to Him, He cannot love us more. And He will not love us less than He already loves us. His love is perfect and constant.

The Bible calls upon us to trust Jesus Christ with our lives and our eternal destiny. It makes no distinction between receiving Him as Savior and Lord. He is both and He is to be received as both. You don't get half of Jesus at one point in your life and wait to receive the other half at a later time.

When you bowed your heart and soul and entrusted your life to Him, you received *all* of Him—Savior and Lord. And He received all of you—your total person.

Once you belong to Him, Jesus calls upon you to obey Him. It won't make Him any more your Lord than it will make Him any more your Savior. But it *will* determine the level of your commitment and the extent of your impact for the cause of Christ.

Whether we like it or not, others are watching our lives. And they are asking some tough questions—a lot tougher than the ones most of us are asking ourselves. They want to know: Is he for real? Does she really know God? Has Christ made a difference in his life? Is He really her Lord?

Our lives speak louder than our lips. People hear what they observe. They are prone to believe what they see. Someone once put it like this: If you were arrested for being a Christian, would there be enough evidence to convict you?

So the question all of us must continually ask ourselves is this: Am I living in obedience to Christ's lordship or am I resisting His rightful authority in my life?

How we answer that simple question will determine the quality of our life. ✳

# 11
~

# Teacher, I Have a Question

*T* *he Pharisees went out and laid plans to trap him in his words.*

Matthew 22:15

Jesus was an incredible teacher. His words overwhelmed His disciples and overpowered His opposition. There was depth to what He said. He was profound, yet simple; powerful, yet practical.

Matthew 22:15-46 records the greatest single confrontation between Jesus and His enemies. In one day He outsmarted them all—Pharisees, Sadducees and Herodians. Each party had its own beliefs, ideas, and practices, and He toppled them all.

The Pharisees were hung up on the Law, so they asked a question about the greatest commandment. The Sadducees didn't believe in things like angels, miracles, and the resurrection of the dead, so they posed a ridiculous question about the resurrection. The Herodians believed in cooperating with King Herod and the Roman officials, so they asked a question about paying taxes to Caesar.

Normally, the Pharisees and Herodians despised each other. Pharisees were strict separatists concerned about zealous adherence to the Law. Herodians were secularists who consorted with Gentiles—eating, working, and playing with them. The two groups were poles apart—except in their opposition to Jesus. So they got together to propose the ultimate dilemma.

"Tell us then, what is your opinion?" they asked the Master. "Is it right to pay taxes to Caesar or not?" (verse 17).

The questioners were attempting to trap Jesus into giving an answer that would get Him into trouble. If Jesus replied, "Yes—pay the taxes," He would offend those who resented the tax. The Pharisees themselves opposed it and Jesus would be exposed as a collaborator with the Romans.

On the other hand, if Jesus said, "No—don't pay the taxes," He would be violating Roman law and the Herodians would report Him to the public officials. He could be arrested for treason and insurrection.

So how did He answer? "You hypocrites," He said. "Show me the coin used for paying the tax."

They handed Him a Roman coin, a denarius. The Romans were proud of their coins; they came with Caesar's image stamped on one side and the official government insignia on the other. They were everywhere throughout the Roman Empire.

"Whose portrait is this? And whose inscription?" Jesus asked His questioners.

"Caesar's" they replied proudly.

And in one swift and simple response, Jesus broke the dilemma. "Give to Caesar what is Caesar's," He said. Jesus treated the coin as though it were of no personal value. "If it is Caesar's coin, then give it back to him; he must need it." We can almost picture Jesus flipping the coin back to them!

"But give to God what is God's," He added. And that is exactly what the Herodians were unwilling to do. They had set their course in life to benefit themselves. They compromised their beliefs to fill their coffers with profits from the Roman government. Taxation. Public projects. New buildings.

But where was God in all this? Left out! They were too busy for Him. Like many of us, they were so busy being busy they had no time for God.

Later the same day, the Sadducees approached Jesus with their question. They had carefully thought it through. The Law of Moses allowed a widow to marry her deceased husband's brother and have children in his honor and memory. So they posed a hypothetical situation: Suppose a widow married her husband's brother and he also died? Suppose there were seven brothers, and they all married her, and they all died?

"Now then, at the resurrection, whose wife will she be of the seven, since all of them were married to her?" they asked smugly. They were sure Jesus could not respond.

They were wrong.

"You are in error," He told them, "because you do not know the Scriptures or the power of God." Now that was an indictment—a double one at that! He then proceeded to show where they erred in their thinking.

"At the resurrection," Jesus explained, "people will neither marry nor be given in marriage; they will be like the angels in heaven" (verse 30).

Angels! The Sadducees didn't believe in angels. What a clever response. In heaven, people will be sexless, like the angels. They will look and act like men and women, but they will not marry in the eternal state.

Then Jesus put the Sadducees on the spot. Clearly they were interested in discussing the resurrection. "Have you not read what God said to you, 'I am the God of Abraham, the God of Isaac, and the God of Jacob'? He is not the God of the dead but of the living," Jesus said, quoting the Sadducees' favorite objection to the idea of the resurrection. If God is the God of Abraham—and no Jew would deny that—then Abraham must be alive. Isaac and Jacob, too!

Jesus' opponents were shocked speechless. They had no argument, no response. Just amazement at His genius.

When the Pharisees heard that Jesus had publicly embarrassed the Herodians and Sadducees, they came to Him next with their own trick question. A theologian asked, "Teacher, which is the greatest commandment in the Law?"

Now, the Pharisees were really hung up on the commandments. For years their scholars had debated how many laws there were and how exactly they were to be followed. Their interpretations eventually became more important to them than the commandments themselves.

Jesus cut through all their legalism and got right to the heart of the Law. "Love the Lord your God with all your heart and with all your soul and with all your mind" and, "Love your neighbor as yourself." These summarized the two tables of the Law: Love to God and responsibility to man—the vertical relationship and the horizontal relationships. "All the Law and the Prophets hang on these two commandments," Jesus added.

Then Jesus turned the tables on the Pharisees and asked them a question: "What do you think about the Christ? Whose son is he?"

"The son of David," they replied, in accord with their belief that Christ (Messiah) would come from the line of David.

"How is it then," Jesus asked, "that David, speaking by the Spirit, calls him 'Lord'?" (Matthew 22:43). Then He quoted Psalm 110:1:

> *The Lord said to my Lord:*
> *Sit at my right hand*
> *until I put your enemies*
> *under your feet.*

"If then David calls him 'Lord,' how can he be his son?" Jesus asked.

No one knew the answer. And from that day on, no one dared ask Jesus any more trick questions!

By the way, what *is* the answer to that last question Jesus asked? Since the Messiah is David's son (his human descendant), how is it that David called him "Lord"? Answer: Because the Messiah is *also* divine! He is Lord *and* God. And Jesus is His name.

There is no greater Savior! ✳

# 12

## Who Is My Neighbor?

*H*e wanted to justify himself, so he
asked Jesus, "And who is my
neighbor?"

Luke 10:29

One of Jesus' most familiar stories is the Parable
of the Good Samaritan. In this story a Samaritan stops
to care for a wounded Jew who has been beaten, robbed,
and left for dead on the Jericho road.

Anyone who has ever visited the Judean
wilderness and traveled down the road to Jericho knows
how desolate a place it is. It's not the kind of place
where you would want to be abandoned all alone. No
trees. No bushes. No shelter. Nothing but barren rock as
far as the eyes can see.

The elevation drops over 3000 feet from
Jerusalem to Jericho in less than 40 miles. The greenery
disappears. The grass soon vanishes. About halfway to
Jericho, you find yourself in a barren, lifeless desert of
sand and stone. Even today, one can't help but feel
overwhelmed by the bleak vista.

Here, in this desolate wilderness, Jesus tells of a Jewish traveler who was attacked by bandits and left for dead on the roadside (Luke 10:30-37). The story was prompted by a discussion of how one might obtain eternal life. A rabbinical expert had challenged Jesus on this point. "Teacher," he asked, "what must I do to inherit eternal life?"

"What is written in the Law?" Jesus asked. "How do you read it?"

The man responded that one should love God with all his heart and his neighbor as himself. In these two responses one can summarize the Ten Commandments, and therefore, the Law itself.

"Do this and you will live," Jesus said.

But the theologian began to quibble over the definition of a person's "neighbor." At the time, some of the Jews limited the commandment to one's *Jewish* neighbor. Samaritans (people who were half Jewish) and Gentiles didn't count.

That is why Jesus deliberately made the Samaritan the hero of the story. In it, two Jews—a priest and a Levite—both pass by the beaten man. They are too busy being religious to notice his wounds or hear his cries.

Whatever else was wrong, the priest and the Levite had their own interests at heart. *Who's got time for this poor soul? Probably some troublemaker. Got what he deserved. Besides, I've got important duties in Jericho. Better keep moving or I'll be late.*

It seems cruel until you put yourself in their shoes. How many times have *you* been on your way to church and observed someone in a crisis? Flat tire. Car broken down. An accident. A robbery. Or perhaps the problem wasn't so obvious. Someone simply had a seemingly insignificant need.

What did you do? Keep on going? Comment on the terrible times in which we live? Shrug the whole thing off? How many times have you walked or driven past someone in need and never given it a second thought?

For whatever reason, both the priest and the Levite passed by the man. Eventually the Samaritan came along, saw him, and took pity on him. He saved his life, bandaged his wounds, and took him to a nearby inn for the night. He paid for the room and even promised to cover any extra expenses while he was away.

Jesus wanted to drive home the point that our love for God parallels our love for people. We love God supremely above all others, but the Bible teaches us that such love never dilutes our love for people. In fact, such love is *expressed* in our love for people.

The Parable of the Good Samaritan is one of the greatest stories Jesus ever told. We can't read it without asking ourselves how many times we overlook opportunities to minister for God.

Such a parable is known as a *juridical* parable because it calls for a verdict at the end of the story. Thus, Jesus' final question: "Who was a neighbor to the man who fell into the hands of robbers?"

The expert in Jewish law couldn't bring himself to say, "The Samaritan." His response was simply, "The one who had mercy on him."

"Go and do likewise," Jesus replied.

Just as Jesus knew the prejudice that existed in the expert's heart and exposed it by making the Samaritan the hero of the story, so also does He expose the prejudice in our hearts as well. Who are the hurting people we pass by? People of another race? Teenagers? Seniors? Unwed mothers? The unemployed? Divorced? Separated? Singles? The poor? The handicapped? The disadvantaged?

Some of us live next door to people we have never bothered to meet. We have never invited them over or taken them to church or even asked them about their relationship to Christ. What are we waiting for? Someone needs us . . . today.

Ask yourself today as you go about your business, "Who is hurting? Who needs my help? Who needs my attention?" Then take time to be a neighbor to him or her in the fullest sense of the term. ✳

# 13

## How Many Times?

*I*f your brother sins, rebuke him, and if he
repents, forgive him. If he sins against you
seven times in a day, and seven times
comes back to you and says, "I repent," forgive
him.

Luke 17:3-4

Jesus understood that life is filled with hurts and
disappointments. And He gave His disciples a simple
plan for dealing with them.

"If your brother sins, rebuke him, and if he
repents, forgive him." Sounds simple enough—but is it
ever tough to do! Notice that the *offended* must take the
first step and rebuke the offender.

You might be thinking, *Why should I have to take
responsibility to resolve this? The offender started it!* True
enough, but we must confront the offense in order to
hold the guilty party responsible. Besides, the person
may not even realize he or she has offended you.

A word of caution is in order. To "rebuke him"
doesn't mean "to blow his head off." Verbal abuse is not
what Jesus had in mind. To rebuke means to be honest.

Tell that person you have been offended by his or her words or actions. Hold that person accountable for how he or she has treated you.

A second word of caution: Give the rebuke in love. Do it in such a way that it encourages repentance. It takes real maturity to give a rebuke properly, and it takes even greater maturity to receive a rebuke properly. Your goal is to resolve the conflict so you can truly forgive and forget the offense.

It works like this:

| *Offender* | *Offended* |
|---|---|
| 1. Sins against you. | 1. Rebukes him. |
| 2. Repents. | 2. Forgives him. |

Make sure you stay on your side of the list. You have two responsibilities if you have been offended: Rebuke and forgive. You can't repent for the other person. Neither can you *make* him repent. Sometimes we think that if we increase the intensity of the rebuke, the offender will get the point and repent. In reality, he may just get mad and walk away.

The disciples had a tough time with the concept of forgiveness. They were raised in a culture that said, "An eye for an eye." They weren't used to the idea of forgiving an offense.

"Lord, increase our faith!" they shouted when they heard this. They were saying, "How in the world can He expect us to do this? Seven times in one day? That's impossible!"

"You already have enough faith," the Savior reminded them. "You just aren't using it." That's what Jesus meant when He said, "If you have faith as small as a mustard seed, you can say to this mulberry tree, 'Be uprooted and planted in the sea,' and it will obey you" (Luke 17:6).

They were believers. They had faith. So what was the problem? They weren't willing to use their faith! Forgiveness involves trust. It means exposing ourselves to hurt, rejection, or misunderstanding. It means being willing to do what is right and trusting God to work it out.

Forgiveness is God's principle, not ours. He makes it work, not us. His Spirit brings conviction to our hearts when we have sinned. We don't have to do it. In fact, we can't!

Our attitude is the key. A person who is being rebuked will immediately sense our attitude. If they think we are being unnecessarily critical or that we are emotionally overreacting, they will not respond well. But if they sense our genuine love, concern, and sincerity, they will be convicted.

Jesus explained this to His disciples in a most dramatic fashion: He told them to take on the attitude of a slave.

"Suppose one of you had a servant," He suggested. Then He described that servant's duties: plowing the fields and tending the sheep. After a long, hard day of physical labor, the servant comes in from the field. Would he sit down to eat before the master eats? No. Rather, he would be required to fix the master's meal first.

Jesus reminded His disciples that the master would not likely thank the slave for his work because he had done what he was expected to do. Then He made the application: "So you also, when you have done everything you were told to do, should say, 'We are unworthy servants; we have only done our duty'" (Luke 17:10).

Those sound like harsh words, but they are not. Our Lord wants us to see that our attitude is the key to our actions. If we are too proud to admit our needs, we won't trust God's advice and do what He says.

Jesus also talked about forgiveness in Matthew 18:15-20. After listening to the Lord, Peter asked, "How many times shall I forgive my brother when he sins against me? Up to seven times?"

Apparently Peter had remembered what Jesus said in Luke 17:3-4. And he wanted to show the Lord that he knew how many times he should forgive: "seven times." But Jesus' reply shocked him.

"I tell you, not seven times, but seventy-seven times," Jesus said.

Seventy-seven times! The King James Version translates Jesus' words, "seventy times seven." That's 490 times! Either way, Jesus meant for us to make a habit of forgiving others.

Forgiveness is not something we do once and that's the end of it. Forgiving is an attitude we have to exercise again and again. It takes practice and we should manifest it throughout our lifetime.

A few verses later, in Matthew 18:23-35, Jesus illustrated the great lengths to which we should be willing to forgive. He told about a servant who owed the king 10,000 talents (several million dollars). When he couldn't pay, the servant begged for forgiveness, and the king granted it. But later, that same servant refused to forgive a fellow servant a debt of a few dollars. Instead of forgiving him, he had him jailed.

The king became angry when he heard this and sent for the servant. "You wicked servant," he said. "Shouldn't you have had mercy on your fellow servant just as I had on you?" Then the king threw him into jail and demanded that he pay all his debt. "This is how my heavenly Father will treat each of you unless you forgive your brother from your heart," Jesus told the disciples.

We don't have a choice when it comes to forgiveness. It is required of God's servants. What's more, it is the evidence that we really *are* His servants.

We who have been forgiven should be glad to forgive. When we forgive others, we confirm what Christ did for us on the cross so that we might be forgiven.

Forgiveness sets us free from hurt, bitterness, and mistrust. It unlocks the sealed heart and sets our emotions free to love, to trust, to grow.

In short: Forgiven people ought to be forgiving people. ✳

# 14

*~*

# Teach Us to Pray

*A*sk and it will be given to you; seek and
you will find; knock and the door will
be opened to you. For everyone who
asks receives; he who seeks finds; and to him who
knocks, the door will be opened.

Matthew 7:7-8

Praying is like breathing. As soon as a child is
born, he or she begins to breathe. Just as breathing is a
sign of physical life, so praying is a sign of spiritual life.
As soon as we are born again, we begin to pray.

But prayer does not come easily. Jesus' own
disciples said, "Lord, teach us to pray" (Luke 11:1). If
they had to learn how to pray, chances are we could use
some lessons, too.

First, Jesus taught them how *not* to pray: "Do not
be like the hypocrites" (Matthew 6:5). Don't show off in
public just to be "seen by men." Our Lord wasn't against
public prayers; the Bible is filled with them. Rather, He
was against showing off. Don't pray to gain the honor of
men. Talk to God; only He can help you. Pray in secret,
and God will answer you in public.

Don't keep on "babbling like pagans," Jesus added ("vain repetitions," the King James Version translates it). That's how the heathen pray. They keep repeating trite, memorized phrases as if their constant repetition will cause God to hear them. But that doesn't impress God. According to Jesus, real prayer must come from the heart. It must be the true expression of your soul.

Jesus taught us a model prayer. Most people call it the Lord's Prayer (Matthew 6:9-13), but because it was a model for the disciples, we should call it the Disciples' Prayer. They were to use it as a guideline for prayer. Ironically, many Christians merely memorize it and repeat it in the same manner He told His disciples *not* to pray.

This model prayer is at once sublime, yet simple. Majestic, yet meaningful. Powerful, yet personal. Like the Ten Commandments, the prayer is divided into our response to God and to our fellow man. The petitions have reference to . . .

God's name
God's kingdom
God's will
    Our bread
    Our debts
    Our foe

Alfred Plummer observed, "The first petition is addressed to God as our *Father*, the second as our *King*, the third as our *Master*. We ask our Father for sustenance, our King for pardon, our Master for guidance."[16]

Jesus taught us to begin by addressing God as our heavenly *Father*. He is not some distant, impersonal deity, removed from our daily lives. He is our Father and He cares about our needs, our problems, and our struggles.

We are to acknowledge Him, praise His holy name, pray for His Kingdom to come, and petition His will to be done. We don't start prayer with our requests. Whenever we pray, we begin with *Him* and *Him alone.*

*Then* we express our needs. As we do, we acknowledge that He alone can meet those needs. We look to Him to provide for us, to forgive us, and to sustain us. The second half of the model prayer is a plea for His grace in every area of our lives.

When we pray this way, we recognize that every gift is from the hand of God. The very cry, "Our Father" acknowledges that we are His children. We need His help. We submit to His will. Those who do not pray in this manner are like children who receive their parents' care and never bother to express their thanks or appreciation.

Prayer is the inner cry of the human heart, the language of the soul that can be heard in the furthermost corridors of heaven. When we pray, we admit who we are, who He is, and that we cannot make it without Him.

What do people do in a crisis? What do they do in the face of death, disaster, and defeat? What do they cry when the bottom falls out and they come to the end of themselves?

"Oh, God!"

It's all they can say. They are at the end of their rope and they can't go on. There is nothing left. Human effort is exhausted; only God can help them now.

Praying is learning to call out to God before it is too late. The sooner we come to the end of ourselves and cry, "Our Father," the better off we will be. Don't wait until tragedy strikes. Don't make God bring you to the edge of disaster before you turn to Him in prayer.

Jesus describes prayer as making a petition, seeking a solution, knocking until you get an answer. Each of those verbs portray deliberate and continuous action. Ask and keep asking. Seek and keep seeking. Knock and keep knocking.

Persistence is the key to getting prayers answered. So is sincerity. God isn't interested in flowery words, proper phrases, or cute clichés. He wants to hear from your heart. He wants you to trust Him enough to express your deepest needs to Him.

Ask Him for His help, guidance, and grace. Seek His will, purpose, and plan for your life. Knock on the door of heaven and keep knocking until God answers.

The promises of God are unlimited. Everything you need is at your disposal in prayer. God's ability to answer and His willingness to help are infinitely greater than your requests. His answers transcend our wildest expectations.

There are only two major hindrances to prayer: sin and unbelief. God will not hear us if we deliberately harbor sin in our hearts (Psalm 66:18). If we "ask amiss" out of selfish desire, God will not grant our request (James 4:3 KJV). If we are unwilling to forgive those who have wronged us, we can't expect God to forgive us (Mark 11:25).

And then there is the matter of faith itself. Unbelief will keep us from asking at all. *Why bother?* we think. *God doesn't care about me. What difference will prayer make?* But Jesus said, "Whatever you ask for in prayer, believe that you have received it, and it will be yours" (Mark 11:24).

Don't pray and expect nothing to happen. Pray in faith, believing God. Expect great things from God because He is a great God. Anticipate the very best from the Savior because there is no greater Savior.

Even when the answer to your prayers is long in coming, keep trusting God for the answer. Charles Spurgeon said, "Frequently the richest answers are not the speediest. A prayer may be all the longer on its voyage because it is bringing a heavier freight of blessing."[17]

God is listening. Trust Him. He knows what He is doing. Keep on calling. Never stop praying. The answer is on the way. ✳

# 15

## Fill My Cup, Lord

*esus answered, "Everyone who drinks this water will be thirsty again, but whoever drinks the water I give him will never thirst. Indeed, the water I give him will become in him a spring of water welling up to eternal life."*

John 4:13-14

He seemed so out of place! A Jewish man sitting on the edge of a well in Samaria. Jews and Samaritans didn't get along very well. What was He doing there?

But she was out of place herself. She had waited until the other women had left before coming to the well. She tried to avoid them as much as she could. Their self-righteous glances, gossipy tongues, and hostile attitudes hardly made her feel welcome.

But there she stood, bucket in hand. In the middle of the day.

Everything was wrong. She was late. She was embarrassed. And now there was a Jew sitting on the edge of the well, right in her way.

"Will you give me a drink?" He asked.

Quite a request for a Jew! They were so fanatical about separation of the races that they usually wouldn't even speak to a Samaritan. Let alone ask for a drink!

"You are a Jew," she replied sarcastically. "And I am a Samaritan woman. Jews do not associate with Samaritans" (John 4:9).

Yet this Jew did. In fact, the Bible indicates He had deliberately chosen this route back to Galilee. Most Jews took the road east of the Jordan Valley so they could avoid Samaria altogether.

Not Jesus. He wanted to go through Samaria. He had business there that wouldn't keep.

"If you knew the gift of God and who it is that asks you for a drink, you would have asked him and he would have given you living water," Jesus said (verse 10).

She was intrigued . . . but still she didn't believe Him.

"Sir, you have nothing to draw with and the well is deep. Where can you get this living water?" she asked.

We can just imagine her looking down the mouth of the well and glancing up at his empty hand.

*Who does He think He is?*

Then came His intriguing reply. "Everyone who drinks this water will be thirsty again, but whoever drinks the water I give him will never thirst."

Jesus was pointing out a contrast between the water in the well and the water He could offer. The benefit of the well water was temporary; the benefit of His water was eternal. She responded instantaneously.

"Sir, give me this water so that I won't get thirsty and have to keep coming here."

She hated coming to that well. It was a lonely trip and she always came *alone.* Somehow it reminded her of the emptiness in her life. She had made some

unfortunate choices in her past and now she was living
with the consequences of those decisions.

Five husbands! It was embarrassing to think about,
let alone explain.

In those days the decision to divorce was usually up
to the husband. Why five men had rejected her we can
only guess. And now she was living with a man to
whom she wasn't married at all. Even by Samaritan
standards, that wasn't an acceptable choice.

It is noteworthy to observe that this particular well
was in the small town of Sychar, near the ancient city
of Shechem in the Samaritan hills. This well—known
as Jacob's well—sat at the base of Mount Ebal. Jacob
had come there nearly 17 centuries earlier to dig the
well. Later, Joshua brought the tribes of Israel there to
pronounce the blessings of God's covenant on nearby
Mount Gerizim and declare the curses of the covenant
on Mount Ebal.

There were twelve curses in all. Four of them had
to do with illicit sexual relations (*see* Deuteronomy
27–28). "You will be pledged to be married to a woman,
but another will take her and ravish her," one of the
curses stated (28:30).

This woman had lived under that curse nearly all of
her adult life. Men had used her and women despised
her. Ravished? She had undoubtedly been abused,
rejected, and discarded. But she couldn't break away
from her addictive pattern.

"Go, call your husband," Jesus insisted, "and come
back."

"I have no husband," she replied.

"You are right," He said. "You have had five
husbands, and the man you now have is not your
husband. What you have just said is quite true."

Jesus' omniscience gave Him an advantage as a counselor. There was no dodging of issues with Him. Why bother trying to cover up the messy details? He knew it all!

Jesus was honest and direct, but also kind. He wouldn't let the Samaritan woman talk her way out of this. Unlike the other men she had known, He really cared about her as a person. He wanted to give her the help she desperately needed.

Jesus deals with all of us that way. He won't accept our excuses or little half-truths. None of them work with Him. He insists that we must be honest before we can get help. He always brings us back to our point of need before He offers us a solution.

The woman knew she had been exposed. "Sir, I can see that you are a prophet," she confessed, perhaps trying to derail Jesus through a compliment. But He wasn't easily influenced by compliments.

Next she brought up a religious debate about whether one should worship in Samaria or in Jerusalem. But He wouldn't buy it.

"God is spirit," He told her, "and his worshipers must worship in spirit and in truth" (John 4:24).

There was something compelling about His words, and something just as compelling about Him. He was unlike any man she had ever met.

"I know that Messiah is coming" she said. "When he comes, he will explain everything to us."

Her faith was so simple, almost naive. Yet, somehow she knew that the Christ would come one day and answer her questions.

"I who speak to you am he," Jesus told her.

It was a shocking declaration. He hadn't told

anyone else He was the Messiah. But he told her. She was the first person to know it.

Not a Jew. A Samaritan!

Not a man. A woman!

Not a saint. A sinner!

He told her that He was the Messiah. He was the answer to all her questions. *And she believed Him.* In fact, she was so overwhelmed she left her water bucket and ran back to town to tell everyone she had found the Messiah.

Charles Spurgeon said, "The heart is insatiable until Jesus fills it. Then it becomes a cup—full to overflowing! Years ago someone said, 'I have been sinking my bucket into the well of grace so often that now I long to put the well to my lips and drink straight on!'"[1]

When this woman reluctantly set out for the well earlier that day, she had no idea she would discover the answer to all her problems. But she did!

You, too, may face such a journey today. It may be something you are dreading. But look carefully as you travel: You are not alone. Jesus Himself sits nearby, waiting to meet your needs. ✳

# Part Three

# What Manner of Man Is This?

---------- ❈ ----------

*They were terrified*
*and asked each other,*
*"Who is this?*
*Even the wind and*
*the waves obey him!"*

—Mark 4:41

# 1

~

# Who Is This Man?

*W*hen *Jesus came to the region of
Caesarea Philippi, he asked his
disciples, "Who do people say the
Son of Man is?"*

Matthew 16:13

No one ever provoked more questions about
Himself than Jesus. The question of His identity comes
up again and again in the Gospel records. Who is He?
Where did He come from? Who do you think He is?
How does He do these miracles?

His own disciples struggled to understand Him,
yet they knew He was no ordinary man. They had seen
and heard too much to believe any less.

Among the people there was no real consensus.
Some thought He was John the Baptist come back from
the dead. Others thought He was Elijah, who had been
taken up to heaven in a whirlwind and whose return
to earth was prophesied in Malachi 4:5. Still others
thought Him to be Jeremiah or one of the other
prophets.

One thing is clear: Jesus was the topic of conversation everywhere in Israel in those days. Nicodemus, a Pharisee, was impressed. The Samaritan woman was convinced He was the Messiah. Nathanael believed He was the King of Israel.

"But what about you?" Jesus asked His disciples. "Who do you say I am?" (Matthew 16:15). He was about to reveal some important truths to them about building His church (verse 18), and there wasn't much use going any further until they settled the question of His identity.

You may have looked at Jesus with an inquisitive glance yourself. Interesting, unusual, unique. Yes, but Who *is* He? Who is He to *you?* Jesus wanted the disciples to settle that question in their minds. And perhaps the time has come for you to do that as well.

"You are the Christ, the Son of the living God," Peter replied on behalf of the others. That was an incredible statement. Let's consider a few facts about Jesus for a moment. And then ask ourselves, "Who is He?"

Jesus was born in a stable where animals were kept. His parents were poor, working-class people. He grew up in an obscure village located in a Roman province. His education was limited to the local synagogue school, yet He mastered the Hebrew Scriptures by the age of 12.

Jesus never wrote a book. Yet more books have been written about Him than anyone else who has ever lived. He never traveled more than 100 miles in any direction. Yet people have traveled to the far reaches of the earth to proclaim His name.

His friends were fishermen and social outcasts, yet He knew no social barriers. He cared nothing for money or material things. He ministered to publicans, sinners, and harlots and still attracted enormous crowds. His teaching was so profound that even the religious experts sat spellbound at His feet. His enemies had to admit there was no rational explanation for His miracles. The blind could see. The lame could walk. The diseased were healed. And the possessed were delivered.

Eventually, however, Jesus' own disciples fled for their lives. One betrayed Him, another denied Him. The rest forsook Him. He died the death of a criminal— reviled, mocked, scourged, crucified. He was nailed on a cross between two thieves and buried in a borrowed tomb.

*Why would anybody believe in Jesus?* Because there was never anyone like Him. In all the history of mankind, no person even comes close to Him. Friends, foes, critics, followers, curiosity-seekers, kings, priests, governors—they all pale into insignificance next to Him.

Jesus is the greatest person who ever lived. His philosophy of life, His morality, His character, and His wisdom all surpass that of anyone else who has ever lived. He, and He alone, stands supreme.

Years ago a man appeared in Chicago, claiming to be Christ. He gathered about 100 followers or so and paraded up and down the streets proclaiming himself to be the Messiah.

In the meantime, Fanny Crosby, the blind hymn-writer, had volunteered to write a new song for the Salvation Army. Shocked that someone would dare claim to be Jesus, she wrote these words: "I shall know Him, I shall know Him, By the prints of the nails in his hands."

That afternoon, the Salvation Army sang her new gospel song on a street corner in Chicago as the false messiah paraded by. Suddenly, a man burst out of the crowd and grabbed the impostor by the hands.

"Look," he shouted, "there are no nail prints! He is a fake!"[1]

Jesus Christ is one of a kind. He is truly unique. There is no one else like Him. Other religious leaders have come and gone, but their teaching cannot compare to His. Their lives may have been unusual, but Jesus stands alone. They lived and died and remain buried, but Jesus lived and died and rose again. No one else ever did that, and no one ever will. He alone is God in human flesh. He alone has the touch of the divine upon His life and ministry. He alone is God!

As you consider the person of Christ, you are compelled to ask, What sort of man is this? Is He really God? Is He the Savior? And as you consider His teaching, you are equally compelled to ask, Is this the truth? Is Jesus the only way to the Father? Is He the answer to all my needs?

Then take it a step further. If Jesus is truly who He claims to be, does He care about me? Does He have a heart for my struggles? Is He concerned about the personal details of my life?

As you read the selections in the pages to come, you will see a Savior like none other. You will encounter someone who is so powerful that He has the power to solve your problems. You will see someone so kind that you will become convinced He cares about you. You will meet someone so loving that you will fall in love with Him.

And you will be convinced of one glorious truth: Jesus not only *is* who He said He is, He also can *do* what He said He can do.

That's why there is no greater Savior! ✳

# 2
~

# Quiet!
# Genius at Work

*H*e got up, rebuked the wind and said to the waves, "Quiet! Be still!" Then the wind died down and it was completely calm.

Mark 4:39

Storms come up quickly over the Sea of Galilee. They blow in from the Mediterranean Sea to the west, sweep over the highlands, and drop down into the lake with little advance warning.

One day while the disciples were sailing on the lake, its calm surface was suddenly churned up by "a furious squall" and the "waves broke over the boat" (verse 37). The rain washed over them and the winds stirred up the waves so that the boat began to fill with water. Yet Jesus slept through the whole thing, snuggled up in the back of the boat—sound asleep! The Ruler of the universe was asleep during the storm. He never was afraid of nature because He ruled both the natural and the supernatural realms.

Even while He was asleep in His human body, Jesus was omniscient. He knew all things. He knew there was a storm and He knew the disciples were afraid. But He never blinked an eye. He wanted them to trust Him in the midst of the storm.

"Teacher, don't you care if we drown?" they pleaded.

Of course Jesus cared about them. But did they care about Him?

"Why are you so afraid?" He asked them. "Do you still have no faith?"

Jesus wanted the disciples to see their panic as a lack of faith. He might have said, "If you really believe I am the Messiah, the Lord of the universe, and the King of Israel, don't you think I can take care of you?"

The wrong kind of fear paralyzes a person and prevents spiritual growth. It stifles progress and impedes justice. Fear keeps us moving backward; it prevents personal progress.

Fear is common to all of us. People suffer from any number of fears:

> Hydrophobia: fear of water
>
> Mysophobia: fear of dirt
>
> Claustrophobia: fear of confined places
>
> Necrophobia: fear of the dead
>
> Nyctophobia: fear of the dark

As long as you are living on planet earth, you are going to face storms. They will come and go and leave their toll. Becoming a Christian doesn't exempt you from problems; they can strike anyone at any time. Difficulty and trouble are a part of our lives, as Jesus Himself warned: "In this world you will have trouble" (John 16:33).

Yet troubles do not have to translate into fears. When Jesus awoke, He rebuked the disciples for their lack of faith. "Do you still have no faith?" He asked. They were in the boat with Him; if He could rest calmly, why couldn't they? But their eyes were on the storm, not on Jesus.

When we focus on the problem, we tend to overlook the solution. Jesus was right there all the time, but they were too busy bailing water to notice. The Master of the universe lay sleeping in the middle of it all. He had it under control all along—but they didn't believe it.

Have your problems ever overwhelmed you? You were sure that no one understood. No one cared. The worst was about to happen and you couldn't do anything about it. Panic set in and faith disappeared.

It doesn't have to be that way. Let faith respond to the challenge and send fear packing its bags. Somebody once said, "Fear knocked at the door of my heart. But when I sent faith to answer the door, no one was there!"

The disciples forgot that Jesus was in the boat with them. The answer was right there; all they had to do was turn to Him. The same is true in your life. If you have received Jesus Christ by faith as your Lord and Savior, He lives within you. He is right there—in all of life's storms. He will never leave you or forsake you.

Jesus is greater than your problems. The Savior who lives within you can conquer any doubt or fear. In *Pilgrim's Progress*, John Bunyan describes the arrest of Christian and Hopeful. The two companions are captured by the Giant Despair and cast into the dungeon of Doubting Castle. Eventually, Christian remembers he has the Key of Promise in his coat. He pulls it out, unlocks the cell, and opens the bars. The two escape to walk again on the King's Highway. So it is with each of us. Claim God's promises and walk by faith, and you will overcome your fears.

Jesus is always as near as your call. All the disciples had to do was call upon Him for help. The solution was right there all along. "Call to me and I will answer you," God promises (Jeremiah 33:3). He delights to hear from us. The sooner you call, the sooner He answers. Hesitation, like fear, is a form of doubt. And doubt will keep you from calling. He wants us to let Him guide every step, every choice, every decision.

At the proper time, Jesus got up and rebuked the storm. "Quiet! Be still!" He commanded, and it stopped. Were the disciples glad and thankful? No; the Bible says, "They were terrified and asked each other, 'Who is this? Even the wind and the waves obey him!'"

The solution to their problem was so dramatic it frightened them. They were stunned. Shocked. Amazed!

The miracle of calming the storm shouts back at us: Jesus is God! He is the sovereign Lord of nature. He is the Creator of life. He is the Sustainer of the world. His spoken word is the final authority over nature itself. Even the winds and the waves obey Him!

It is no wonder the disciples were in awe of Jesus. His was no mere human power. He was not some magician who was good at sleight of hand. He could do miracles by just speaking a word. After all, if He spoke the world into existence, He could surely tell it to quiet down when it acted up!

After the sea grew calm, the disciples sat in reverent silence while the boat sailed across the smooth waters. They thought they had seen His power at its best. And they were impressed. But little did they realize what lay ahead. ✳

# 3

## He Touched Me

*Everywhere he went . . . they placed the sick in the marketplaces. They begged him to let them touch even the edge of his cloak, and all who touched him were healed.*

Mark 6:56

You could see the boat coming in the distance, gliding across the silvery smooth waters of the Sea of Galilee. As soon as Jesus and the disciples landed at Gadera and stepped out on the shore, someone recognized Him.

"It's Jesus of Nazareth!"

Word spread quickly through the village. Soon people were rushing out to greet Him. A ring of excitement was in the air. Someone brought a sick friend to be healed, then another. Soon the marketplace was filled with hurting people lying on mats.

Imagine what it must have been like to be there as Jesus walked by. Picture yourself lying on a mat in the marketplace. You gaze upward and your hand stretches out toward Him. *A miracle! I need a miracle!*

But there were so many people . . . everywhere. The crowds were so thick that it was almost impossible to get near Him.

*If only I could touch the edge of His garment as He passes by. I believe. I really do believe. Yes . . . yes . . . something's happening! I feel different . . . I'm being healed! Completely, totally—it's a miracle!*

It happened again and again, everywhere He went. People looked up, recognized Him, and reached out by faith to touch Him. And they were healed. Instantly. Miraculously.

Even the most hardened skeptics cannot deny that Jesus had a reputation as a healer and miracle-worker. There is no other explanation for His popularity and the great crowds that followed Him.

But what about today? Does Jesus still perform miracles? Can I, too, reach out and touch Him? Will He do a miracle in my life?

Yes, He will. But first you must recognize who He is. Mark 6:54 says, "As soon as they got out of the boat, people recognized Jesus." Before they could place their trust in Him they needed to know Him. Once they were convinced it was He, they knew what they had to do.

Faith is only as valid as the object of that faith. If you trust your car to start up in the morning but it has no engine, it will not start. Sincere faith in a faulty object produces only frustration.

The Bible urges us to put our trust in Jesus Christ. He is to be the object of our faith. And when He is, miraculous things begin to happen. Lives are changed. Sins are forgiven. Bodies are healed. Families are reconciled. Habits are broken. People are set free.

But not only must we recognize who Jesus is, we also must reach out to Him by faith. People came to Jesus seeking His help. They did not let pride hold them back. They knew they had problems and they were willing to bring them to Jesus. Hundreds came—the poor, the outcast, the hurting. They all came, just to get a glimpse of the Savior.

They were *hearing* people. They were willing to listen to His call. As word spread among them that Jesus was coming, they believed it. The sick heard it. Their friends heard it. Their relatives heard it. And they all came to listen to Jesus.

They were also *honest* people. Nobody had to prod them to acknowledge their needs. They were desperate; they knew they needed help. That's why they came to Jesus.

Last, they were *humble* people. Their needs were so great, they were beyond pride. As long as we think we can solve our own problems we will go right on trying to do so without God's help. But when we finally come to the end of ourselves, we admit that we have nowhere else to turn but to Him.

These desperate people were humble enough to let their needs be exposed so they could get help. No social pretense. No prideful cover-up. "Here I am. Just as I am. All my problems, difficulties, limitations, and heartaches—exposed for all to see."

I wonder . . . are you listening to God's call? Do you have a need that only He can meet? What is He telling you to do about it? Are you willing to do it?

Honesty is difficult for some of us. Honesty makes us uncomfortable because it makes us so vulnerable. But it also makes us face reality. It makes us admit our needs. And only then will we reach out to the One who can meet our needs.

As people reached out to touch Jesus' garment, they were healed. He had the power to help them, but they had to realize it and act by faith. They were like the woman who had been bleeding constantly for 12 years. She was convinced Jesus could help her. She said to herself, "If I only touch his cloak, I will be healed" (Matthew 9:21).

Keep in mind that people were crowded around Jesus, bumping and pushing. Arms, legs, elbows, knees. The woman probably had to struggle to touch Jesus. She finally got close enough to reach Him from behind and touch Him by faith. "Who touched me?" Jesus asked as He turned around.

"Touched you?" the disciples wondered out loud. "There are scores of people touching you. The crowd is all around us."

But there was only one person that moment who realized her need and touched Jesus *by faith.* She was startled at first when He turned toward her. He seemed disturbed, but He wasn't. He was pleased that she realized He could help her.

"Take heart, daughter," He said, "your faith has healed you" (Matthew 9:22). That very moment she was miraculously healed.

Perhaps you are struggling with something painful in your life. You have tried every way possible to correct it. But you are still struggling. Are you at the end of your rope? Why not turn to Jesus with it? Reach out by faith to Him. Just touch the edge of His garment— that's enough. God will do the rest. ✳

# 4

## Where Demons Fear to Tread

*W*hen he saw Jesus, he cried out...
*"What do you want with me, Jesus,*
*Son of the Most High God? I beg you,*
*don't torture me!"*

Luke 8:28

Luke chapter 8 takes us to the other side of the
Sea of Galilee to a remote place near the Golan
Heights. There, Jesus and the disciples were greeted by
desert-like conditions, steep precipices, and barren cliffs
dropping down toward the field at the water's edge.

Upon stepping ashore, the group encountered a
demon-possessed man. He was a wild man, running
around naked in the countryside, and living in the
tombs—an outcast, a maniac, a child of the devil. But
also, apparently, a Jew.

Gadara, the region of the Gerasenes, wasn't
exactly an orthodox Jewish community. It lay on the
edge of Gentile territory, which probably explains why
they were keeping pigs there. No orthodox Jew would
have lived near such "unclean" animals, but the

Gerasenes were willing to overlook a few encroachments to the Law.

The whole scene is bizarre. The wild man (often called "the demoniac") was himself "unclean"—living among the dead ensured that. And living in naked filth sealed it. The pigs grazing nearby on the hillside were also considered unclean. In fact, the Jews considered the whole area unclean. But Jesus went there anyway.

The boat's arrival caused a stir of excitement and the madman ran out to see what it was all about. No doubt he made a habit of showing up at public events, always making a nuisance of himself. The townspeople had tried to chain him up, but he always broke loose. This time, however, would be different. This time his tormented soul would come face to face with the Son of God.

When the demoniac saw Jesus, he fell to his feet and began screaming, "What do you want with me, Jesus, Son of the Most High God?" The demons knew who Jesus was and they knew they were powerless in His presence. This incident ought to be reassuring to everyone who has ever felt demon oppression. The demons were helpless! They begged and squealed and pleaded. They cowered in Jesus' presence.

There is no record of the disciples saying one word during this encounter. They had already been amazed by Jesus' power over the natural world; now they would see a demonstration of His power over the supernatural.

"I beg you, don't torture me!" a voice called from within the man.

"What is your name?" Jesus demanded.

"Legion," the voice replied, meaning there were *many* demons in him. They then begged Jesus not to cast them into the abyss.

This is where the pigs enter the story. Some Gentile or backslidden Jew kept a herd of pigs nearby. Now remember, Jews weren't supposed to keep pigs, eat pork, or even touch swine. But there they were, feeding on the hillside.

The legion of demons begged to be sent into the pigs. That may seem like a strange request, but the demons saw it as a better option than the abyss. "Don't send us into eternal condemnation yet," they were saying. "It's not yet time." No, but that time is fast approaching!

Jesus commanded the demons to come out of the man and they entered the herd of pigs. When they did, the herd became violent and stampeded down the cliffs, plunged into the lake, and drowned.

Destructive devils! They destroy everything they touch. Their goal had been to destroy the young man, but Jesus set him free. Now the young man was completely changed. The Bible describes him as "sitting at Jesus' feet, dressed and in his right mind" (verse 35). Deliverance! Transformation! That's what Jesus does when we come face to face with His power and authority.

You would think the local people would have been thrilled. Yet the Bible says when they saw the man so dramatically changed, they became afraid and begged Jesus to leave. They weren't used to this; He scared them to death. So Jesus got back into the boat and left.

Their reaction really isn't so surprising as it might sound. How many times have you been afraid to turn everything over to God? You came right up to a certain point and then backed off. Why? You knew what it would cost. It would mean total surrender, and you weren't willing.

Think of it: You could have been set free long ago. But you wouldn't accept His will in the matter. It still hasn't worked out, has it?

Isn't it time to let Jesus take over? Stop making excuses and denying the problems. Face up to reality and surrender to his lordship and authority.

You can't read this story without being amazed by the power and person of Jesus. He not only commands the wind and waves, but demons tremble in His presence as well! They acknowledge their own defeat and pronounce their own doom. They don't even put up a fight.

Then why are we so afraid of demons? Because we focus on our weakness instead of God's power. We see our shortcomings and invite further defeat. "Go ahead, I can't resist," we might as well say.

But we are *in Christ*, and in Him is all the power we need to resist the enemy. Victory over temptation does not come by trying harder, living better, or being more disciplined. Satan's forces can defeat our most valiant efforts. That is why we are not the answer. Jesus is!

Jesus has won the battle for us. He has met Satan face to face and won. The tempter was banished. The Savior was victorious. And He continues to win our fights for us. As David recognized in the Old Testament, "the battle is the LORD'S" (1 Samuel 17:47). The New Testament adds, "We are more than conquerors through him who loved us" (Romans 8:37).

Jesus will set you free if you ask Him. But He won't if you don't. Choose the latter option, and you will keep on running around in a frenzy until you come to the end of yourself. When you finally do, you will find Jesus was there all the time. Waiting for you to come to your senses.

Waiting for you to come home. ✳

# 5

## Guess Who's Coming to Dinner?

*ere is a boy with five small barley loaves and two small fish, but how far will they go among so many?*

John 6:9

The Feeding of the 5000 is the only miracle (except for the resurrection) recorded in all four Gospels. It left such a deep impression on the disciples that they never forgot it.

The incident occurred during springtime at the height of Jesus' Galilean ministry, one year before the crucifixion. Picture yourself on a green, grassy hillside overlooking the blue waters of the Sea of Galilee. Mountains ring the lake, adding a perfect backdrop to the scene.

Mark mentions that the Seventy had just reported back from their preaching tour, and all four Gospels note Jesus' remorse over the recent death of John the Baptist. We then read that the Master took the Twelve and departed to a lonely place. They needed a break, a chance to get away from it all. It was time to go where they would not be bothered. But it didn't work that way.

As soon as people realized where the group was going, thousands began running to the spot. David Redding says, "The Great Physician was no sooner in the boat than He saw His patients mobbing His vacation spot."[2] How did Jesus react to this interruption? Luke 9:11 says, "He welcomed them and spoke to them about the kingdom of God." Matthew 14:14 tells us, "He had compassion on them and healed their sick."

What an incredible Person! We always see Him with a heart for others. Most of us would have been upset or at least frustrated. But not Jesus. He reached out to people and met their needs.

Even the disciples couldn't take it. By the end of the day they were saying, "Send the crowd away" (Luke 9:12). It was late. They were in a remote place. John 6:4 notes it was near Passover and the people had already begun removing the bread from their homes in preparation. Besides, they had come spontaneously to this remote area. No one had thought about dinner.

Except one boy, the kid with the five loaves and two small fish. His mother had probably packed this meal for him. God bless her! Neither she nor the boy could have imagined what Jesus would do with it.

The Lord turned to Philip, who was from that region. "Where shall we buy bread for these people to eat?" He asked, testing Philip's faith. *You've got to be kidding!* Philip must have thought. *Get serious!* "Eight months' wages would not buy enough bread for each one to have a bite!" he responded.

What do you think you would have said? Now, don't be so pious; most of us would have said the same thing. The disciples were relatively poor and didn't have enough money to feed such a crowd.

What's interesting is that no one suggested a miracle; that wasn't even up for discussion. After all, Satan had tried to get Jesus to turn stones into bread once before and He had refused. Satan tempted Jesus to do a miracle to benefit Himself and He said, "No!" But this was different. Jesus wasn't thinking about Himself; He was thinking about thousands of hungry people.

Now, in the Gospels, we see that Andrew was always bringing people to Jesus. This time he brought the boy with the lunch. "Here is a boy with five small barley loaves and two small fish, but how far will they go among so many?" he asked (John 6:8).

This wasn't much, but it was a start. At least Andrew was trying. Five flat little barley loaves and a couple of sardines. It wasn't even a man-sized meal. A kid's lunch was all they had.

And that was all Jesus needed.

Once you are willing to turn your meager supplies over to Him, He will multiply your efforts beyond your wildest dreams. Once your inadequacy is touched by His power, it becomes more than adequate in His service.

Can't you just see Jesus as He tenderly reaches down to receive the boy's lunch? There is no indication the boy ever hesitated. The Bible says, "Jesus then took the loaves, gave thanks, and distributed to those who were seated as much as they wanted. He did the same with the fish" (John 6:11).

It was a miracle of multiplication. The Lord had the disciples divide the crowd into groups of 50. They sat them down on the grass and organized the distribution process. Jesus broke off pieces of bread and fish and gave the food to the disciples. They, in turn, broke off pieces to give to the people.

Every time Jesus tore off a piece of bread, there was still as much left in His hand. The more the disciples distributed, the more there was. In fact, by the time they finished feeding 5000 men (and who knows how many women and children), they had more left over than they started with. Twelve baskets of leftovers... one for each disciple.

Jesus made the disciples clean up the leftovers. No littering the countryside or wasting God's provisions. Orderliness, delegation, responsibility, generosity, and frugality. The story is loaded with character, decency, and compassion.

But the crowd took all this the wrong way. "Surely this is the Prophet who is to come into the world," they said. They were referring to Moses' prediction in Deuteronomy 18:15. They were ready to take Jesus by force and make Him king.

That is when Jesus "withdrew again to a mountain by himself" (John 6:14). That night He went where no one else could find Him. He walked across the water to the other side.

Charles Swindoll observes the balance between Jesus' humanity and His deity in this incident. On the one hand, we see Jesus in prayer, which underscores His humanity. "Deity has no needs," Swindoll states. "Prayer is an act of mankind. Humans pray. . . . And in praying Jesus shows himself human."[3] But then He turns around and walks on water. Only God walks on water, and in so doing we see His deity.

Here is a Savior who cares, who prays, who cries, who feeds the hungry. He is fully human and understands our needs. But then He is also fully divine, the God-man. He walks on water, heals the sick, feeds the multitude, works miracles.

But beyond it all, He has a message He wants us to hear: "I am the bread of life," He cried (John 6:35). "You only need Me!" He was explaining. The crowd had returned looking for more bread—"manna from heaven," they called it—but the real gift from heaven was Jesus Himself. He was the "living bread" (John 6:51). And He was all they needed.

He still is. ✳

# 6

~

# A Little Faith Goes a Long Way

When the disciples saw him walking on the lake, they were terrified. "It's a ghost," they said, and cried out in fear. But Jesus immediately said to them, "Take courage! It is I. Don't be afraid."

Matthew 14:26-27

The feeding of the 5000 had ended. The disciples packed up and got into a boat to cross the lake. In the meantime, Jesus dismissed the crowd and went up into the hills to pray alone. By nightfall, the disciples found themselves struggling with the boat against high winds.

As they wrestled with the sails some distance out in the water, they thought they could see a figure approaching them. Someone...something...was walking across the water toward their boat, and they cried out in fear.

They were scared to death. "Phantasma!" they screamed. A ghost! A spirit! A phantom! It never occurred to them that this might be Jesus.

"Don't be afraid," He called to them. "It is I."

The Master? Walking on the water? How? Critics have proposed every imaginable solution. Shallow water. Unseen rocks under the surface. An apparition. An imaginary episode. A myth? No... a miracle!

The Gospel account wipes out all objections. The boat was far out into the lake. It's deep there—no sand bars, no rocks. Just plenty of water.

"Lord, if it's you," Peter shouted, "tell me to come to you on the water" (verse 28).

"Come," Jesus replied.

Full of enthusiasm, Peter got out of the boat and walked on the water toward Jesus. A double miracle! But as Peter ventured from the boat, he began to look at the wind and the waves, and he began to sink.

Drowning men don't have time for long prayers. Peter's consisted of just three words: "Lord, save me!" But that was enough. Jesus reached out, caught him, and took him back to the boat.

"You of little faith," Jesus said to Peter. "Why did you doubt? (verse 31).

By the time they got into the boat, the disciples were on their knees worshiping Jesus. "Truly you are the Son of God," they proclaimed. "No one ever did that before; You must be divine!"

Peter sat there, soaking wet. While the others may have laughed at him, he had done something none of them dared try—he had walked on water. Someone observed that He got a dunking for his daring, but at least he dared the impossible. And for a few moments, he succeeded.

Several principles are taught in this story, but one of the most important ones reminds us of the sovereign intervention of God in our lives. He doesn't wait for us to come to Him; He comes to us in the midst of our struggles. He is the seeking Savior. He is out looking for the lost, the helpless, the hopeless.

When you feel like you can't find your way to Him, just wait. He will find His way to you. Even in the midst of life's storms, He comes to us in all of His power, walking on the waves.

That is so characteristic of Jesus. There is nothing mediocre or second-rate about Him. He does everything in a big way. No mistake about this miracle; it was typical of Jesus. He could command the forces of nature and conquer the forces of hell. He could reverse the curse of sin, cure disease, heal the sick, and raise the dead.

Walking on water was no problem for Him. It was just an evening stroll, a shortcut across the lake. But a very well-timed shortcut. He arrived at just the moment the disciples needed Him most.

Jesus is always on time. Did you know that? Jesus specializes in miracles of timing. He loves doing things just at the right moment. Turning water into wine, feeding the multitude, healing the sick, raising the dead—always at precisely the right moment. The Lord of life is also the Lord of time. No matter how dire your situation, Jesus knows what time it is in your life.

"But I can't wait much longer," you say. Jesus will be right there, just when you need Him the most. He has an unsurpassed sense of timing. Don't panic. He always delivers—on time. Jesus is always on duty, whether in the middle of the day or the deep of night. He's always there. Listening. Waiting. Available. Just when you need Him.

Greg Laurie makes this observation:

> Don't think this diligence is hap-
> hazard! Jesus always acted according to a

plan. . . . He had an agenda, a plan, a
schedule. There were no accidents.
Everything transpired according to His
perfect plan. The Master had appointments
to keep, settled long ago in the counsels of
eternity, and He was never late.[4]

Even today, Jesus calls us where none dare to go.
"Come," He said to Peter, inviting the disciple to walk
on the water with Him. Most of us would have stayed in
the boat. But Peter launched out. Good old, impulsive
Peter. They could always depend on Peter to liven things
up.

Eyes transfixed on Jesus, Peter climbed out of the
boat and stepped on the surface of the water. Before he
knew it, he was walking toward his Lord. Maybe he
didn't get very far, but he tried. That's more than the
others did. They just sat there, huddled up together. But
Peter went for the walk of a lifetime!

We can't duplicate the powerful works of our
Savior. But we *can* do things for Him that are beyond
our wildest imagination. We, too, can step out by faith
and go where none have dared to go.

God may be calling you to serve Him in a special
capacity. He may be calling you to a full and complete
surrender of your life to Him. He may be calling you to
sing, teach, preach, counsel, evangelize, encourage, or
minister. Answer His call! Say yes to Him.

One of the grandest privileges of life is to know
that you are living in the center of His will, doing what
He has called you to do, going where He is sending you
to serve.

Of this you can be certain: He will go with you
every step of the way. ✳

# 7

*~*

# Watch Your Attitude

*esus turned and rebuked them. And he said, "You do not know what kind of spirit you are of, for the Son of man did not come to destroy men's lives, but to save them."*

Luke 9:55-56 (margin)

Attitudes determine almost everything about the character of our lives. It has often been said: *attitude determines altitude.* You will rise only as high as your attitude. People with negative attitudes prevent their own rise to greatness.

Jesus spent a disproportionate amount of time dealing with the attitudes of His disciples. In some cases they were slow learners; it seemed as if they would never get the point.

Such was the case with a series of events recorded in Luke 9. The chapter ends with one of the Savior's most stern rebukes: "You do not know what kind of spirit you are of." How did the disciples get in such a mess? It all began with pride.

*Inflated spirit.* Jesus sent the Twelve on a

preaching mission that turned out to be extremely successful (Luke 9:10). They preached the gospel and healed the sick. They were doing what Jesus had been doing, and they got good at it. That's how the trouble all started. They came back bragging on their success. They couldn't wait to tell the Master what *they* had accomplished (verse 10). They were so full of themselves that He took them out of the public eye and retreated to Bethsaida to refocus their perspective.

*Uncompassionate spirit.* Luke tells the story of the feeding of the 5000 in just a few verses. In the middle of the chapter, he records the discussion about Jesus' identity. Then Luke adds the statement around which the whole chapter pivots: "If anyone would come after me, he must deny himself and take up his cross daily and follow me" (9:23).

There it is—the key to their attitude problem. They were full of themselves and hadn't denied themselves anything. They certainly weren't living the crucified life; their attitudes showed it. When we nurture too high an opinion of ourselves, we tend to get too low an opinion of others. We can't be full of ourselves and have a heart for someone else.

*Indifferent spirit.* Next, Luke mentions the transfiguration (9:28-36). What a glorious event! The veil of flesh was torn away and Jesus stood resplendent in His glory—shekinah glory! God's glory! It was the ultimate revelation of His deity. And what were the disciples doing? Sleeping. They fell asleep at the transfiguration. What indifference! The inner circle—Peter, James and John—had all fallen asleep.

*Impotent spirit.* While Jesus and the three disciples were on the Mount of Transfiguration, the other nine disciples were attempting to heal a demon-possessed boy back in the town below (9:37-40). The boy's father had brought him to the nine but they failed miserably. We can only assume they said whatever they thought they were supposed to say and they did whatever they thought they were supposed to do, but nothing happened.

At last Jesus, Peter, James, and John arrived. "I begged your disciples to drive it out," the boy's father explained, "but they could not." They were impotent, powerless . . . failures. They must have stood there looking sheepish and embarrassed.

"Bring your son here," Jesus said. While the boy was coming toward Jesus, the demon convulsed within him. The boy went into a seizure and fell to the ground, but Jesus rebuked the evil spirit and healed the boy. The disciples sure couldn't do it; they didn't have the right spirit within themselves.

*Immature spirit.* Unbelievably, in the next scene we see the disciples arguing among themselves about who was the greatest (9:46). Imagine—they had just slept through the transfiguration and had failed to heal the boy. And now they were arguing about who was the greatest? But that's human immaturity. The disciples were concerned about rank and position, pecking order and seating arrangements. They were especially preoccupied with who would sit next to Jesus in heaven.

The Lord knew what they were thinking, so He took a small child and had him stand beside Him. Then Jesus said, "He who is least among you all—he is the greatest" (verse 48). The disciples were shocked. Children were at the bottom of the social ladder in those days. Most people paid them no attention at all.

*Inconsistent spirit.* Like most self-centered people, the disciples were totally inconsistent. "Master, we saw a man driving out demons in your name and we tried to stop him, because he is not one of us" (verse 49). *How could God use such a person?* they no doubt thought. They couldn't believe he was using Jesus' name. He wasn't even one of the Twelve! Who did this guy think he was, anyway?

"Do not stop him," Jesus scolded, "for whoever is not against you is for you." You need all the help you can get, Jesus told them. Don't reject the help of other believers. And don't think you are the only people who know Me. God's family is bigger than you think it is.

*Intolerant spirit.* Luke ends the chapter with the final expression of the disciples' wrong attitudes (9:51-56). This was the straw that broke the camel's back—the incident that caused Jesus to turn and rebuke them severely.

The Lord was on His way from Galilee to Jerusalem and sent messengers ahead to tell the Samaritans He was coming. The Samaritans had been receptive to His ministry and perhaps He felt obligated to stop there. But when they realized the nature of His journey, they urged Him to keep going to Jerusalem.

James and John ("the Sons of Thunder") took this as a personal insult. They felt rejected and came to Jesus, asking, "Lord, do you want us to call fire down from heaven to destroy them?"

No grace. Just judgment. Give them a blast from the past, just like Elijah. Lightning bolts from heaven. Fry them to the glory of God!

"No!" Jesus shouted in a stinging rebuke. "You do not know what kind of spirit you are of, for the Son of Man did not come to destroy men's lives, but to save them."

We are not here to kill people, Jesus explained. My mission is to save, not destroy. I have come to redeem the lost, not bring judgment.

For three years Jesus worked on the disciples' attitudes. Just when it looked like they were making progress, they would suddenly regress. Even at the Last Supper on the night before the crucifixion, they were still arguing about who was the greatest and where they were going to sit in the coming kingdom.

We tend to read these accounts and divorce ourselves from them. We tell ourselves we would never act as the disciples did. Yet all too often, we are just as overconfident as they were—and just as inconsistent and judgmental, too.

This may be a good time for an attitude check in your own life. If it's true that your attitude determines your altitude, how high would you be flying right now?

If your attitude needs some work, let God take over. Fortunately for us, He is at His best when we are at our worst. ✳

# 8
## ~

# The Latest Dirt

*esus bent down and started to write on the ground with his finger. . . . "If any one of you is without sin, let him be the first to throw a stone at her."*

John 8:6-7

There she was, sprawled on the pavement at Jesus' feet. Publicly exposed. Morally naked. Spiritually defiled. Caught in the very act of adultery during the festivities of the Feast of Tabernacles.

Of course, the whole thing was a setup by the Pharisees. They didn't care about her at all. They were only using her to set a trap for Jesus.

And what an ingenious trap it was—the perfect dilemma. There seemed no way out of this one. Jewish law demanded the death penalty for adultery, but Roman law forbade the carrying out of this punishment.

"Teacher," they said to Jesus, "this woman was caught in the act of adultery. In the Law Moses commanded us to stone such women. Now what do you say?" (John 8:4-5).

If Jesus says, "Stone her," the Pharisees can incite the crowd to do the dirty work. Then, when the Roman soldiers arrive to deal with the mob, they can simply blame her death on Jesus and the Romans will execute Him. On the other hand, if He says, "Don't stone her," He will violate the Law of Moses. Then the Pharisees can denounce Him as a heretic and hope the crowd will stone Him. Either way, they win and Jesus dies.

They miscalculated, however. They forgot with whom they were dealing.

This was no ordinary rabbi, no would-be, self-appointed teacher. This was the *Savior*, and there was never anybody else like Him. Here we see Him at His best. His keen insight breaks the dilemma by putting the choice back on the accusers. He exposes their true motives and runs them off without an argument. He defends morality by forcing everyone in sight to make a moral choice.

This story is so powerful that some have questioned its authority. Some early manuscripts dropped it altogether. Even today, some translations question it. But it fits perfectly into the context and sets the stage for the upcoming discourse on the Light of the world (verse 12ff.) William Hendriksen says, "The Christ as pictured here is entirely 'in character' as he is . . . also pictured elsewhere."[5] Leon Morris writes, "The story is true to the character of Jesus. Throughout the history of the church, it has been held . . . that it is authentic."[6]

There is no doubt the woman was in serious trouble. Why did they pick her? And where was the man? We can only speculate. But there she was, dragged out in public for all to see.

We know little else about her. Was she married? Single? Divorced? Was it a first offense? A lifelong pattern? A momentary lapse? All we know for sure is that she was guilty. She had been caught.

Just like you.

You may not have sinned like she sinned, but you have sinned. And you, too, stand accused by that sin. There is no way out of it. All of us have been caught and condemned. "All have sinned and fall short of the glory of God" (Romans 3:23). "There is no one righteous, not even one" (Romans 3:11).

We, too, have been slapped down on the pavement of life. We are naked before the world in all our sin, accused by Satan himself both day and night. "Death!" he keeps screaming. "They deserve death! The penalty for sin is death!"

The Bible reminds us, "The wages of sin is death" (Romans 6:23). The Scripture minces no words. It tells it like it is. We have all sinned, we stand condemned, and we all deserve to die—just like the woman in our story.

"Now what do you say?" the Pharisees demanded of Jesus. They wondered how He would try to get out of this one. But Jesus had no time for their dirt. Instead, He went straight to the dirt itself—the very substance from which we are all created. He bent down and wrote in the dirt with His finger.

Everyone speculates at this point. What did He write? A list of other sins? The sins of the Pharisees? The Ten Commandments? No one knows; the Bible never says. In fact, the real significance is not in *what* He wrote but *that* He wrote!

He turned His back on the accusers, the religious elite. You just didn't do that in Jewish society. It was an act of disgust. He refused to answer their question because He knew what was in their hearts: envy, jealousy, greed, and murder.

When Jesus stooped down, He got on the woman's level. He cared deeply about sinners and here was a sinner in need of a Savior.

After a few moments of silence, Jesus straightened up and said to her accusers, "If any one of you is without sin, let him be the first to throw a stone at her."

His brilliant answer broke the dilemma and yet upheld the morality of the Law. It also exposed the evil intent of the Pharisees. Jesus defended the legitimacy of the moral law, but by offering her accusers an opportunity to cast the first stone, He placed the responsibility for her execution in their hands. Then He stooped down and wrote on the ground again with His back toward them.

One by one they realized their little scheme had failed. If anyone was going to violate Roman law that day, it would have to be the Pharisees, and they weren't about to do that. So one by one, they left. Defeated. Humiliated. Overwhelmed by the greatest mind in history.

But wait a moment—the woman was still there, exposed, accused, humiliated. And the crowd was still there, watching, wondering, questioning. *What will He say to her?*

That's what it all comes down to for each of us. What will He say to me? Will He condemn me? Will He demand the ultimate penalty? Will it cost me everything?

Turning to her, Jesus asked, "Woman, where are they? Has no one condemned you?"

"No one, sir," she answered.

"Then neither do I condemn you," Jesus declared. "Go now and leave your life of sin" (John 8:11).

What mercy! What grace! What forgiveness! What pardon! What a Savior!

Jesus alone could pronounce her guiltless because He alone would take her sin and nail it to His cross. He alone could let her go free because He alone could free her from bondage.

Picture yourself as that woman. Sinful. Condemned. Helpless. And then picture yourself in front of Jesus, face to face. What will He say to you? The same thing He said to her. "Neither do I condemn you." The Bible expresses it this way in Romans 8:1: "There is now no condemnation for those who are in Christ Jesus."

The woman found out that day what sinners are still finding out today. Jesus loves us more than we deserve, and He forgives us more than we dare ask. ✳

# 9

## Who Do You Think You Are?

*I*f *you do not believe that I am the one I
claim to be, you will indeed die in your
sins. . . ." "Who are you?" they asked.
"Just what I have been claiming all along," Jesus
replied.*

John 8:24-25

Who are you? This question dominates the
Gospel accounts. And it still dominates virtually every
discussion about Jesus Christ in modern times. Carl
Henry said, "Nowhere is the tension . . . focused more
dramatically than in the conflict over the identity of
Jesus of Nazareth."[7]

Who was He? A prophet? A great teacher? A
spiritual leader? A wild-eyed radical? A troublemaker?
Or was He really the Son of God? People wanted to
know the answer to those questions back then even as
now.

Nowhere in Scripture is this more obvious than
in the discussion between Jesus and His critics in John
7–8. He goes to Jerusalem during the Feast of Tabernacles and His presence sets off a fierce debate over His

identity. "Surely this man is the Prophet," some conclude. Others claim, "He is the Christ."

"Yes, you know me, and you know where I am from," Jesus declares (7:28). The whispers increased in number throughout the crowd: "Who is He? Is He the Messiah? Is He the King of Israel?"

Those whispers can still be heard today. Take your Bible and scan John chapters 7–8. Soon you will find yourself asking the same questions, seeking the same answers. Who is He? Who does He claim to be? Can I believe Him? Can He really make a difference in my life?

The whole city of Jerusalem was abuzz. Everybody was talking about Jesus and anticipation was running high. Had the Messiah actually come? Would He now set up His kingdom on earth?

The chief priests, however, had heard enough. They sent the Temple guards to arrest Jesus. But as the guards listened to Him teach, they were awestruck. Spellbound. Dumbfounded. Helpless. Speechless. They returned empty-handed with the memorable explanation, "No one ever spoke the way this man does" (7:46).

But then Jesus had the audacity to proclaim that He was the "light of the world" and that He could turn people from darkness to light. This made the Pharisees more upset. "Who do you think you are?" they shouted.

"I am not alone," Jesus replied. "I stand with the Father who sent me" (8:16).

"Where is your father?" they asked.

"You do not know me or my Father," Jesus replied.

You won't read a more confrontational conversation anywhere. Jesus asserted that He was the son of the Father, making Himself the Son of God. The Pharisees denied His testimony, questioned His sanity, and rejected His authority.

"You are from below," Jesus explained. "I am from above. You are of this world; I am not of this world" (8:23). He couldn't make the distinction any more clear. But still they didn't get it. How could He be standing there looking so human and still claim to be from heaven?

This question divided the audience. Some believed on Him. To them He said, "You will know the truth, and the truth will set you free" (8:32). To them, He was the Great Liberator. But to others, He said, "You belong to your father, the devil" (8:44). To them, He was a madman. "Demon-possessed," they called Him.

The whole discussion revolved around the issue of identity—His and theirs. "We are Abraham's descendants," they insisted. They claimed they were in bondage to no one and they didn't need to be set free. But they were in bondage—bondage to sin. They needed the spiritual freedom Jesus had to offer them.

"The reason you do not hear is that you do not belong to God," Jesus told them (8:47). After that, the conversation moves back and forth 12 times between Jesus and His critics. "Your testimony is not true!" "You are a Samaritan!" "You are demon-possessed!"

John chapter 8 highlights the tension. The people love Him but the religious leaders hate Him. They won't even consider the possibility that He is who He claims to be—and you can be sure they understood His claim. Don't think they missed the point. They got it loud and clear.

The debate finally came down to Jesus claiming to be the Son of God and the Jews claiming to be the sons of Abraham. To which Jesus said, "Your father Abraham rejoiced at the thought of seeing my day; he saw it and was glad" (8:56). Abraham saw the coming of the Messiah prophetically with the eye of faith.

But the leaders couldn't see it. "You are not yet fifty years old," they said to him. "And you have seen Abraham!" The patriarch had lived 2000 years before their time; how could he possibly know about Jesus? Who did Jesus think He was anyway?

"I tell you the truth," Jesus answered, "before Abraham was born, I am!" (8:58).

*That* did it. "I AM" was the name by which God disclosed Himself to Moses at the burning bush. Every first-century Jew knew immediately what Jesus meant. That's why they picked up stones to put Him to death— for blasphemy. But He escaped.

Have you ever read a book or news article where some modern author writes that Jesus never claimed to be God? Don't believe it! John 8 is filled with such claims. Jesus let people know that He was greater than Abraham (the Father of the Jews) and Moses (the giver of the Law). He supersedes them both! Why? Because He is God.

Look at His life. Listen to His words. Examine His claims. Watch His relationships. He is love in action, wisdom personified, deity on foot. Jesus Christ is God!

We have only two choices. Bow down and worship Him, or pick up stones and execute Him. Either He is God and deserves our worship, or He is an impostor and ought to be stoned. You decide. Bow your head, or grab your stone. Which will it be?

If Jesus really is who He claimed to be, He deserves our worship, our life, our all. ✳

# 10

*~*

# Seeing Is Believing

*H*e replied, *"Whether he is a sinner or not, I don't know. One thing I do know. I was blind but now I see!"*
John 9:25

Healing the blind was Jesus' specialty. It was one of His most dramatic miracles. And it takes on greater significance when we remember there is not one such miracle in the Old Testament. No prophet, priest, or king ever gave sight to the blind. None! Not Moses. Not Elijah. Not Elisha. Not Isaiah. No one!

In the Old Testament, giving sight to the blind is associated only with the ministry of the coming Messiah (Isaiah 29:18; 35:5). Thus Jesus' ability to perform this miracle is one of the greatest proofs that He is the Messiah. In fact, the Gospels record more miracles of healing the blind than any other kind of healing Jesus did.

The Bible makes it clear that only Jesus can heal the blind. It also makes it clear that He did it often. The only other reference to healing blindness was connected with our Lord's appearance to Paul on the road to Damascus. Paul was struck with temporary blindness until Ananias touched him in Jesus' name (Acts 9:17).

But Jesus came to do more than give sight to the blind. He came to give *spiritual* sight to those who were spiritually blind. Nowhere is that more evident than in John 9, where the man born blind receives both physical and spiritual sight. Let's take a closer look at what happened.

As Jesus and the disciples were walking along the streets of Jerusalem, they encountered a man who had been born blind. "Rabbi, who sinned," the disciples asked, "this man or his parents?" It was common in those days to assume that all personal tragedies were the result of someone's sin. Either the blind man brought it on himself or he was suffering because of the sin of his parents.

"Neither," Jesus replied. "This happened so that the work of God might be displayed in his life."

We may be reluctant to believe it or hesitant to grasp it, but all personal failures and human disasters are *opportunities* for the power of God to be displayed in our lives. No matter what we may be going through right now, God can and will be glorified through it. His grace will be sufficient, His name glorified, and His power displayed.

Sickness, disease, and infirmity ultimately result from sin in general. They are the consequences of a fallen world. But they are not necessarily the result of individual sins. Don't think that every time you get sick it is because you did something wrong.

Most of the time, Jesus healed people merely by speaking. But in John 9, He healed the blind man with the help of spit. We are not told why, but it is interesting to note that saliva was believed by the ancients to have healing powers. For instance, what do you do when you cut your finger? You put it in your mouth. The ancients also associated a person's spit with his words.

Jesus spat on the ground, made moist clay, and anointed the man's eyes. He then told the man to go to the Pool of Siloam (*Siloam* means "sent") to wash off the clay. The man did so, washed off the clay, and came home seeing.

The miracle was instantaneous. As soon as the man washed away the clay, he could see. For the first time in his life, he saw the sky, the grass, flowers, people, and everything else around him. His family and friends were shocked and amazed.

"How . . . were your eyes opened?" they asked.

"The man they call Jesus," he replied. But he had lost track of Jesus and didn't know where to find Him.

Now there is a hitch in the story. The miracle happened on the Sabbath, a fact which infuriated the Pharisees. "The healer cannot be of God," they proclaimed. "He must be a sinner—He violates the Sabbath." Such a statement reveals that the Pharisees loved the Sabbath more than they loved God.

"How can a sinner do such miraculous signs?" the people asked.

"We know this man is a sinner," the religious leaders insisted.

Then the man who had been healed said, "Whether he is a sinner or not, I don't know. One thing I do know. I was blind but now I see!"

You don't have to be a theologian to receive a miracle. The man had a lot to learn about Jesus, but he did know one thing—he could see!

When the Pharisees kept asking him more questions, the man finally asked what they were really after. "Do you want to become his disciples, too?" He also found it remarkable that they couldn't say where Jesus' power came from. "You don't know where he comes from, yet he opened my eyes," he said. "We know that God does not listen to sinners. . . . If this man were not from God, he could do nothing" (9:30-33).

This was not exactly what the Pharisees wanted to hear. They blew up and threw the man out—excommunicated him right on the spot. Gone! Farewell! Outta here!

At just that point, Jesus went and found him—just like He finds us when we are abandoned. It doesn't matter how lonely or rejected you feel, Jesus knows right where you are. You're not alone; He is on His way to retrieve you even now. He specializes in redeeming the lost, the rejected, the outcast. He really cares. And He won't leave you all alone.

"Do you believe in the Son of Man?" Jesus asked.

"Who is he, sir?" the man asked.

"You have now seen him," Jesus replied. "In fact, he is the one speaking with you."

"Lord, I believe," the man said, and fell down and worshiped Him.

What a precious sight! The blind man could see, for the first time, the One who had healed him. And he fell down on his knees and adored Him.

And Jesus let him do it. He let the man worship Him because He is God.

What would you have done? Imagine you were born blind and a man gave you your sight and told you to believe in Him. Anybody with *any* sense would believe and worship Him.

But Jesus came to give more than physical sight. He came to set us free from spiritual darkness. He came from the splendor of heaven to the midnight of earth.

He came from glory itself that we might be set free from the darkness of sin. No wonder He cried out, "I am the light of the world."

Has Jesus set you free? Has the glory of His presence penetrated the dark recesses of your soul? Have you been delivered from the kingdom of darkness? Are you walking in the kingdom of light?

If you have come to know Jesus personally, you too have received spiritual sight. When He enters our lives, His Spirit initiates new life and new sight. Being born again is like having a light turned on in your soul. As the light of Christ's presence fills your life, the spiritual darkness of your heart is dispelled. A dramatic change takes place. God is there, the light has come, and Jesus lives within!

Jesus deserves our heart and soul, our life and devotion, our worship and service. In a word, our all in all. Does He have yours? ✳

# 11
~

# No Thanks

*Jesus asked, "Were not all ten cleansed? Where are the other nine? Was no one found to return and give praise to God except this foreigner?"*

Luke 17:17-18

Jesus, the Healer, was coming. He was traveling along the border between Galilee and Samaria. As He came upon the village, ten lepers approached Him. Then they stopped, keeping their distance, and called out to Him.

"Jesus, Master, have pity on us!" they cried.

Leprosy is a terrible disease. It numbs the skin, turns it to flakes, and can even lead to the gradual loss of a person's fingers, toes, hands, and feet. It was considered one of the most dreaded diseases of the ancient world. Lepers were virtual outcasts from society.

These ten lepers apparently congregated together. Rejected by family, friends, and foes alike, lepers were desperate people. They could not be readmitted into society unless the Temple priests pronounced them cleansed or cured. Without this approval, lepers remained in a hopeless state.

These ten lepers came to Jesus, desperate for His help. There was no internal debate or lengthy discussion. They heard He was coming and they knew He was their only hope. There they were, on the edge of town—pitiful, dressed in rags, and wrapped in bandages. All they could do was call out for mercy.

They came to the right person! Jesus' compassion was so great He could not turn people down. He could not walk past the hurting without helping. His love reached out to them again and again. He had the power to heal them and He had to use it.

"Go, show yourselves to the priests," Jesus told them, and they did. They didn't stand there arguing with Him. They had made a request: "Have pity on us." And He responded with a command: "Go, show yourselves to the priests."

The Bible says that the lepers were healed as soon as they obeyed: "As they went, they were cleansed" (Luke 17:14). They were healed en route, while they were in the process of obeying. They were cleansed in traffic on their way to the Temple.

Each of the ten lepers was cleansed. Jesus spoke, they obeyed, and they were cleansed. It was all that simple. Instantly, as they walked along, they were healed of their dreadful disease. Imagine their excitement! Their joy! Their happiness!

One of them returned to Jesus to thank Him. Praising God in a loud voice, he threw himself at Jesus' feet. But where were the other nine? Apparently they were too busy reveling in their healing. They got to rejoicing so much they forgot to be grateful.

"Were not all ten cleansed?" Jesus asked. "Where are the other nine?" Ten lepers were healed, but only one came back to say thanks. The other nine were so excited about their healing they forgot the Healer. They got caught up in their blessings and forgot the Blesser.

How many times have we done the same thing? We were so captivated by the Savior's goodness that we forgot the good Savior. We ran off telling everyone *what* He had done and not *who* He is.

"Where are the other nine?" Jesus' words of incredulity still ring down through the corridor of time. The other lepers never did come back. They were gone and they weren't about to return. They were too busy being blessed to give a blessing.

Jesus missed them, too. He realized immediately what they had done. No one came back but one. And he was a Samaritan! The Jews took Jesus for granted; only the foreigner returned to say "thank you."

Somehow we are compelled to believe that the Samaritan, used to rejection, was most grateful for pardon. And he went home blessed: "Rise," Jesus told him. "Your faith has made you well." There was something permanent in those words, something reassuring.

If your own healing depended on your attitude, would you be healed? If your gratefulness determined the nature and extent of your miracle, would you have one? If your obedience affected your disposition, would it change for the better?

These are just a few of the many questions we could ask ourselves. Each one brings us closer to an understanding of ourselves, our attitudes, and our values. Whenever we are too busy to say thank you, we are just plain too busy. Nothing is more important than gratitude. It expresses our appreciation for His grace, His love, His mercy.

We aren't told what happened to the nine lepers who never came back. How selfish! How ungrateful!

How unthinkable! Now, reflect back on your own experiences for a moment. How many times have you gone to a pastor, teacher, counselor, or doctor for help? After you got better, did you send a note? Pay a visit? Drop by just to say things were going fine?

I hope so, but I fear many of us will have to admit that we didn't. We, too, rushed off to count our blessings . . . and forgot to be a blessing.

It's never too late to change. Think of someone today who has been used of God to touch your life. Take a minute to call or write. Stop by, if you can, and just say, "Thanks."

Don't be like the nine. Be like the one. And remember, gratitude is the recognition of God's grace in our lives. ✳

# 12

## Set Free!

*O*n this rock I will build my church, and
the gates of Hades will not overcome it.
Matthew 16:18

Have you ever gone to church and asked
yourself:

"Why are we here?"

"Where is God in all this?"

"Is this what Jesus really intended to establish?"

"Does the church really have a future?"

Don't become worried if these kinds of thoughts
come to your mind. Such questions are healthy. They
force us to look at things more honestly and they
provoke us to find answers.

To be sure, the good old "Ship of Zion" has had her
foes without and her failures within. She has had to
navigate through the depths of persecution and the
shoals of prosperity. She has had to make her course
through shifting cultures and changing times. Yet, she

sails on. Her flag unfurled, her course set, her destiny certain.

The church plays a paramount role in the New Testament:

> Jesus announced it and established it.
>
> He died on the cross for it.
>
> He rose from the dead for it.
>
> He commissioned it to evangelize the world.
>
> He empowered it with His Spirit.
>
> He promised to build it and sustain it.
>
> He promised to come again for it.
>
> He plans to make it His bride.
>
> He will return with her at His side.

When Jesus got ready to make His announcement about the church, He took His disciples to Caesarea Philippi, a Gentile city named after Caesar. It was far to the north, near the borders of Israel, Lebanon, and Syria. To His Jewish disciples it must have seemed an inappropriate place for such an announcement.

But to Jesus, it was the perfect place. A Gentile city. A Greco-Roman city. Here He would announce His intention to form a church that would eventually embrace Gentiles as well as Jews—a church for all people. Regardless of race, nationality, or ethnic origin, it would be a truly universal and international assembly of believers.

The Greek New Testament word for "church" is *ekklēsia*. This term comes from two Greek words. *Ek* means "out" (like our word *exit*). *Klēsia* comes from the verb *kaleō*, "to call." Simply put, *ekklēsia* means "to call out" or "to assemble." Thus, the basic idea of a church is a group of people called out of the world and assembled unto Jesus Christ. We are His assembly, His congregation, His church.

When Jesus asked the disciples who they thought He was, He was seeking a confession of faith. Some people thought He was John the Baptist or Elijah, but the disciples believed He was "the Christ, the Son of the living God" (Matthew 16:16). That is the essential core of truth upon which Jesus would establish His church.

Peter spoke up and made the confession on behalf of all the apostles. Jesus replied, "I tell you that you are Peter, and on this rock I will build my church." Now, the rock on which the church would be built was not Peter or the other disciples. It was their confession of faith, which rested in Him. Ephesians 2:20 explains it this way: The church is "built on the foundation of the apostles and prophets, with Christ Jesus himself as the chief cornerstone."

The New Testament describes the church as a *building*, a Holy Temple made up of living stones and assembled by the great Master Builder (Ephesians 2:21). It also describes the church as a *body*, a coordination of various members who work together for the good of the whole (Romans 12:4). And Jesus is pictured as "the head of the body, the church" (Colossians 1:18).

When the Lord Jesus announced the establishment of the church, He also predicted its progress. "I will *build* my church," He said. The verb is a progressive future in the original Greek text. It means, "I will *continue* to build." And so He has.

From its announcement by the rocky cliffs at Caesarea Philippi to its empowerment on the Day of Pentecost and its eventual spread across Asia, Africa, Europe, and the New World, the church of our Lord

Jesus Christ has grown into the most widespread, international organism on earth.

Some time later, in His prophetic message on the Mount of Olives, Jesus would amplify this same truth. "This gospel of the kingdom," He predicted, "will be preached in the whole world as a testimony to all nations, and then the end will come" (Matthew 24:14). Jesus would amplify this again in His "Great Commission" (Matthew 28:19-20). He commanded, "Therefore go and make disciples of all nations. . . . And surely I will be with you always, to the very end of the age."

Perhaps the most incredible part of our Lord's announcement about the church is the proclamation that "the gates of Hades will not overcome it." The King James Version says, "the gates of hell shall not prevail against it."

We tend to read that statement and picture hell on the attack and the church on the defensive. But a person does not *attack* with gates; he *defends* with gates. So in reality, Jesus pictures the church on the attack and the kingdom of Satan on the run!

*Hades* represents the whole of Satan's domain: death, the grave, and hell itself. Christ's death and resurrection will break the power of Satan, the god of this world. Jesus will triumph over His foe and He will enable His church to do the same.

It isn't the church defensive, but the church *militant*. It must not be the church passive, but the church *aggressive*. It will not be the church defeated, but the church *triumphant!*

The kingdom of Satan is no match for the true church of Jesus Christ. As the gospel is preached and the lost are converted, the power of Christ prevails. People are snatched out of the gates of hell and set free by the power of the gospel.

Those of us who make up the church are no longer citizens of darkness, but citizens of the light. We are no longer held in chains of bondage; we have been released. We are no longer reserved unto judgment; we have a destiny with the King of kings. Jesus has won our freedom and broken our bonds. He has set us free!

Jesus has also given us the "keys of the kingdom of heaven" (Matthew 16:19). We have not only been released, but we also have the great privilege of releasing others. As we proclaim His gospel, we announce His power. As His word goes forth, His Spirit convicts us and convinces us that He is indeed the Christ, the Son of the living God, the Savior of the world.

Which leads to a final question: If the church is so important to Jesus Christ . . . shouldn't it also be important to those who claim His name? ✳

# 13
~

# We Shall
# Behold Him

*esus . . . led them up a high mountain. . . .
There he was transfigured before them.
His face shone like the sun, and his
clothes became as white as the light.*

Matthew 17:1-2

The transfiguration is one of the most
spectacular events in the life of Christ. It is the only
display of His divine glory recorded in the Gospels. For
a brief moment, three of His disciples saw Him in the
splendor of heaven itself. They saw Him as He really is,
the divine Son of God.

Man has always had difficulty with God's glory.
Moses could see it only in a reflected form. The Ark
of the Covenant covered it. The Veil of the Temple
obscured it. The Holy of Holies contained it. When
men dared invade it, they paid with their lives.

What the disciples saw that day on the
mountaintop was deity on display. They already knew
Jesus was no ordinary man. His miracles were proof
enough of that. They had seen Him heal the sick, feed
the multitudes, cast out demons, and walk on water. But

in all those situations, He looked like a man. His humanity was always before them. He walked, talked, lived, and rested like a man. But on this special day, Jesus looked like God.

When most of us picture Jesus in our minds, we see the *human* Jesus—the teacher, the prophet, the healer. We rarely think of Him in His glorified form. We don't see Him like the disciples did that day or like John saw Him years later on Patmos, where "His head and hair were white like wool, as white as snow, and his eyes were like blazing fire" (Revelation 1:14).

Have you ever thought of Jesus in the fullness of His glory? It is hard for most of us to picture Him in His deity. We can comprehend Him walking, talking, preaching, teaching. Yet we have difficulty comprehending His deity because we are not divine. Theologians refer to this as the *incomprehensibility* of God. We know enough about Him to know Him. But we cannot know all there is to know because He is beyond our full comprehension.

Jesus took the inner circle of the disciples—Peter, James, and John—with Him. They climbed a high mountain alone while the other disciples remained in the valley below. The others did not see the magnificent sight—and the three who were there almost missed it! Luke 9:32 tells us the three were exhausted and nearly slept through the whole thing.

As incredible as it may be, think of how often we sleep through the very moments of God's greatness. He is about to do something significant, the power of His Spirit is about to move. But we are exhausted from the activities of the day and we want to stop when God wants to move on. We want to relax when He wants to stir us up.

You may be exhausted. Weary from life's responsibilities. Tired out. Worn to a frazzle. You may be thinking, *I just can't go on!* You may feel as if you've had all you can take. But at your very moment of weakness, God wants to put His power on display in your life.

During the transfiguration, Moses and Elijah appeared with Jesus. Moses represented the Law; and Elijah, the Prophets. Together they symbolize the entire Old Testament. Awakening from his sleepiness to see this amazing sight, Peter suggests they build three tabernacles—one for Jesus, one for Moses, and one for Elijah. But at that moment, God began to speak: "This is my Son, whom I love; with him I am well pleased. Listen to him!" Suddenly, Moses and Elijah vanish and Jesus is left alone.

When the three disciples realized the full significance of what was happening, they fell on their faces. They were terrified. Awestruck. Speechless in the presence of God, helpless before His majesty, powerless before His glory.

Never think you can approach the Lord casually. No one ever has. Even His own disciples fell prostrate before Him when they realized who He was. Years later, when Christ appeared to John on Patmos, virtually the same scene was repeated. He came in His glory and John hit the ground, terrified.

"Get up," Jesus said. "Don't be afraid." His words were calming and reassuring, just as they always are when He speaks to us in our moments of crisis. He always rises to the occasion, saying just what we need to hear, just when we need to hear it.

If you are going through a difficult time—if you feel like falling down and giving up—remember: Jesus will be there for you just when you need Him most.

It is interesting to note that the term *transfigure* comes from the Greek word *metamorphoō*, from which we get our English word *metamorphosis*. It speaks of a total transformation. Not only was Jesus transformed before the disciples' eyes, but He is also in the business of transforming us. As soon as Christ enters your life, that transformation begins. You become a "new creation" in Christ (2 Corinthians 5:17).

As believers, we share in Christ's transforming power in two ways: 1) We are personally and spiritually transformed at the moment of salvation; and 2) we will be ultimately and permanently transformed in heaven in the eternal and glorified state.

Think of it: Each one of us who have received Christ into our lives will be transformed by His life. We have been changed by the indwelling Spirit of Christ, who lives within us. Theologians call that transformation *regeneration*, or the new birth. To be born again is to be spiritually transformed by the regenerating power of Christ.

Now, let's take this thought one step further. If Christ can transform our spiritual nature for all eternity, He can also transform us on a daily basis. His transforming power is inexhaustible. It is without limits. It goes on and on, as long as we need it. The Scripture urges us, "Do not conform any longer to the pattern of this world, but be transformed by the renewing of your mind" (Romans 12:2).

There's the key! Transformation affects the heart, soul, and mind. It changes the inner being of a person. It affects a change in our thinking. Our minds are renewed by Christ's presence. We not only *become* Christians by faith, we begin to *think* like Christians as we are transformed by the Spirit of Christ.

"Can I be a Christian but not think like a Christian?" you may ask. Certainly! None of us think Christianly *all* the time. On any given Monday morning you may wake up knowing you are a Christian and feeling like you are a Christian, but by the time you've spilled your milk, burnt your toast, forgotten your briefcase, and been stuck in traffic for 60 minutes, you may no longer be thinking like a Christian. You may not even be talking like one!

That's why we all need Christ's transforming power *daily* in our lives. Renewal is a day-by-day process. It starts with conversion, at the moment we are regenerated and born again into the family of God. But it continues throughout our spiritual journey. As long as we are on earth, we will need daily transformation to meet the challenges of life.

Perhaps your car won't start. Maybe you don't feel good, or the kids are sick. Or your boss is upset, or the business is struggling. Perhaps your bills are due and you don't know how you'll pay them. You feel like you just can't take anymore.

When all the pressures and problems of life mount up against you, remember that God is still there. He's ready and willing to take your burden, share your sorrow, and transform your life. Day by day. Difficulty by difficulty. Problem by problem.

Wake up and take a good look. There He is, in all His glory, splendor, and power. What a Savior! He can do for you what you cannot do for yourself. ✻

# 14

~

# Good Grief!

*esus said to her, "I am the resurrection
and the life. He who believes in me will
live, even though he dies. . . . Do you
believe this?"*

John 11:25-26

Lazarus was one of Jesus' best friends. So were
his sisters, Mary and Martha. They were committed
followers of Christ and He often stayed in their home in
Bethany on the outskirts of Jerusalem. Galileans were
welcome there, and Jesus and the disciples accepted the
hospitality gladly.

By the time we reach John chapter 11, however,
opposition was rapidly rising against them. That's
why Jesus and the Twelve retreated across the Jordan
River, deliberately avoiding the region of Judea. When
the message came that Lazarus was seriously ill, Jesus
seemed hesitant to respond. Returning to Judea meant
jeopardizing their own lives.

But that wasn't the reason Jesus kept from
acting. His delay was deliberate. He knew He had to
wait for certain events to take place, so He stayed across

the Jordan for two more days before making the journey to Bethany.

"This sickness will not end in death," the Savior promised. "No, it is for God's glory so that God's Son may be glorified through it" (John 11:4).

Jesus knew that Lazarus had died, no doubt even before the messenger had arrived. Yet He also knew that He must delay His journey. There had to be absolutely no doubt about the finality of Lazarus's death, especially in light of what the Lord intended to do when He got to Bethany.

"Our friend Lazarus has fallen asleep; but I am going there to wake him up," Jesus explained (verse 11).

The disciples didn't understand. Why wake him if he sleeps? He needs his rest, doesn't he?

"Lazarus is dead," the Lord finally explained. "And for your sake I am glad I was not there."

*Glad?* You let Your friend die? What kind of friendship is that? The disciples must have been totally unnerved.

"Let us also go," Thomas suggested, "that we may die with him." *That* was a desperate idea! Let's all just die and get it over with. The disciples didn't have much fight left in them.

By the time they arrived in Bethany, Lazarus had been dead for four days. Family, friends, and mourners filled the house. Martha and Mary were brokenhearted. Someone whispered to them through their tears that the Master had finally come. Martha got up and went out to meet Him, but Mary was so distraught she remained in the house.

We cannot fully comprehend the deep hurt and pain these women were experiencing. They were grieving because their brother had died, but they were also in agony because their Lord had let them down.

Surely He could have healed him. He healed so many other people, some of whom were total strangers. Surely He could have saved His friend!

Have you ever reached such a point? The bottom fell right out of your life. And you thought, *Why, God? Why me? Why now?* Suddenly life didn't make sense. Even God didn't make sense.

James Dobson has warned, "Unfortunately, many young believers—and some older ones too—do not know there will be times in every person's life when circumstances don't add up—when God doesn't appear to make sense. This aspect of the Christian faith is not well advertised. We tend to teach new Christians the portion of our theology that is attractive to a secular mind."[8]

Pain affects each of us differently because we aren't all wired the same way. Martha had the gift of serving. She was emotionally reserved, strong, determined, organized, efficient. She reacted with disappointment and she met Jesus with a rebuke: "If you had been here, my brother would not have died" (verse 21). She might as well have said, "You're late! Where have You been?"

On the other hand, Mary had the gift of mercy. She was emotionally expressive, loving, passionate, empathetic, caring. She reacted with despair, and when she finally did come out of the house to face Jesus, she fell at His feet and sobbed. Moved by her tears, the Scripture simply says, "Jesus wept" (verse 35). The term used in the original Greek text means that He "burst into tears." He sobbed with her.

"Your brother will rise again," Jesus told Martha.

"I know he will rise," she replied, ". . . at the last day." That is, in the future. At the end of time. In the final resurrection.

Then Jesus looked Martha right in the eyes. There was something dramatic about Him. He was captivating, commanding, and compassionate all at the same time. "I am the resurrection and the life," He said. "He who believes in me will live . . . [and] never die." Then He looked even deeper into her eyes. "Do you believe this?" He asked.

"Yes, Lord," she replied. "I believe that you are the Christ, the Son of God."

Notice that she did not say, "I believe You can raise my brother." Her confession was greater than that. By affirming that He was the Messiah, the Son of God, she was saying, "I believe You can do anything. I believe in *who* You are, not just in *what* You can do."

Jesus then asked Mary, "Where have you laid him?"

Taking Jesus by the arm, the weeping sisters made their way to the tomb. His heart ached for them and for all mankind. The sting of death had penetrated their lives and they were deeply hurt. The agony of the curse of sin had claimed another victim, leaving broken hearts in its path. But the Savior, who would walk that path Himself, took them under His arms and wept with them as they walked to the grave.

The Bible says, "During the days of Jesus' life on earth, he offered up prayers and petitions with loud cries and tears" (Hebrews 5:7). There is no Savior like Him! He loves us and cares for us with a love that is beyond human comprehension. His grace is more than sufficient. His mercy is unlimited, His love amazing, and His compassion knows no bounds.

When the threesome arrived at the stone sealing the burial cave, Jesus was again deeply moved. Perhaps He saw a very similar scene just a few days off—women weeping at a stone-covered tomb, helpless to do anything but cry.

"Take away the stone," He demanded.

"But...he has been there four days," Martha protested.

"Did I not tell you that if you believed, you would see the glory of God?" He asked.

Jesus personified God's glory on earth. The disciples actually saw it on the Mount of Transfiguration. And now they would see it in a different way.

After the people rolled away the stone, Jesus called out in a loud voice: "Lazarus, come out!"

And then it happened! The dead man came up, walking out of the tomb, still wrapped in his burial shroud.

"Take off the grave clothes and let him go," Jesus said.

Our Lord has been saying that ever since. Every time someone is born again by faith in Jesus Christ, he or she is released from the power of death and resurrected to new life in Christ. A "new creation" is enabled to enjoy the gift of life forever. Truly, "the old has gone, the new has come!" (2 Corinthians 5:17). ✳

# 15

# The King Is Coming

*ay to the Daughter of Zion, "See, your king comes to you, gentle and riding on a donkey, on a colt, the foal of a donkey."*
Matthew 21:5

The King is coming . . . on a donkey! Just like the past kings of Israel. The Son of David rode down from the Mount of Olives, past Gethsemane, across the Kidron Valley, and through the Eastern Gate.

The triumphal entry of Christ into Jerusalem marked His official presentation as the Messiah. So dramatic was this event that all four Gospels mentioned it.

Thousands of people followed Jesus, all waving palm branches, the symbol of royalty. They lined the road with their cloaks and shouted, "Hosanna to the Son of David!"

Jesus' ride into Jerusalem fulfilled the biblical prophecy: "Your King comes to you . . . gentle and riding on a donkey" (Zechariah 9:9). He came like a Jewish King—humble, simple, powerful. There was no

elaborate ceremony, no Roman general on a white
horse, no marching army.

Jesus was the people's choice. They welcomed Him,
shouting, "Hosanna" (which means "save us"). They
added, "Blessed is he who comes in the name of the
Lord" from Psalm 118:26. He was their Messiah. And
they had waited so long for Him to arrive.

The whole city was fascinated. Passover was coming
and visitors were already crowding Jerusalem for the
festivities. So thousands of people were on hand when
Jesus came to Jerusalem for the last time. He had been
there before, eight days after His birth to be presented
at the Temple. He came again when He was 12 years
old, amazing the scholars. And He came again when He
began His ministry and healed the sick.

But this time was different. He came riding into
the city dramatically, publicly, like an Old Testament
king from the House of David. Everyone saw Him and
they all wanted to know, "Who is this?"

"Jesus, the prophet from Nazareth," was the reply.

He made His way straight to the Temple, where He
healed the sick, gave sight to the blind, and made the
lame to walk. Then He threw out the money changers.

"My house will be called a house of prayer," He
said. "But you are making it a 'den of robbers.'"

Jesus was resolute, captivating, and powerful. No
one stood in His way. Even the children cried out,
"Hosanna to the Son of David!"

Yet not everyone was enthralled. "Teacher, rebuke
your disciples!" the Pharisees demanded (Luke 19:39).

"If they keep quiet," Jesus replied, "the stones will
cry out."

But even in Jesus' triumph there was tragedy. The
Bible tells us He wept as He entered the city. "If you,
even you, had only known," He lamented. "You did not

recognize the time of God's coming to you" (Luke 19:42,44). God had come in the Person of His Son. While the people welcomed Him, the leaders rejected Him. He was to be the stone the builders of religion rejected. But God would make Him the cornerstone of the new Temple—the church of the living God.

During all the commotion, some Gentiles requested to see Jesus. In contrast to the Jews who rejected Him, these Gentiles came seeking Him. They approached Philip and Andrew, the only disciples with Greek names. "We would like to see Jesus," they said (John 12:21).

When the disciples relayed the request to Jesus, He immediately announced: "The hour has come for the Son of Man to be glorified" (John 12:23). He knew that His time had come. Israel's rejection would soon be complete and His reception by the Gentiles would begin.

"Now the prince of this world will be driven out," Jesus declared. "But I, when I am lifted up from the earth, will draw all men to myself" (John 12:31-32).

Everyone who lived in the Roman Empire knew what "lifted up" meant—crucifixion. That horrible Roman method of execution. *Crucified? The Messiah? But we thought He would live forever. How can this be?* the people wondered.

Many questions swirled in their heads. Jesus just let them swirl. He had other things to do, places to go, people to visit, disciples to minister to. So He disappeared. And there the people stood with all their unanswered questions.

The Puritan, Thomas Watson, said, "God is to be trusted when His providences seem to run contrary to His promises."[9] God promised David a crown, but he spent years in exile before he received it. The Lord promised Paul deliverance from the storm, but the ship ran aground and split into pieces. And it was upon those very pieces of the ship that the sailors were all delivered.

God's timing is always perfect. It may not appear that way to us because ours is a limited and finite view. But His is an eternal and omniscient view. He sees the end from the beginning and He already knows how the last chapter will be written. So He knows exactly how to time His answers to our requests. John Flavel wrote, "Grace makes the promise and providence the payment."[10]

Ironically, the story of Jesus' triumph ends in tragedy. His official presentation as Messiah leads to His official rejection by the nation of Israel. John hints at it early in his Gospel when he writes, "He came to that which was his own, but his own did not receive him" (John 1:11).

His own people rejected their Messiah. They turned against their King. "Crucify him!" they would soon shout. "Let his blood be on us and on our children!" they insisted (Matthew 27:25). And it was!

But before we are too quick to condemn the Jews for their unbelief, we ought to examine ourselves. How many times have you said no to Him? How often has He convicted your heart about some detail in your life only to hear you say, "Let me be"?

We, too, face the constant decision: Do we accept Him or reject Him? Do we acknowledge His claim on our lives? Or do we refuse to let Him have control? Will we obey? Or will we disobey?

Decisions, decisions. You cannot consider the Person of Jesus Christ without making some serious decisions. If He really is the Son of God, when will I decide to give myself to Him? If He really is the Savior of the world, when will I invite Him to be *my* personal Savior? If He really is Lord and King, when will I bow my knee to His lordship? And when will I crown Him King of my life?

When the King comes again, will He be coming for you? ✳

# Part Four

# Surely This Is the Son of God!

———— ✳ ————

*The centurion and those with him
. . . were terrified, and exclaimed,
"Surely he was the Son of God!"*
—Matthew 27:54

# 1
~

# Broken and Spilled Out

*M*ary took about a pint of pure nard,
an expensive perfume; she poured it
on Jesus' feet and wiped his feet with
her hair. And the house was filled with the
fragrance of the perfume.

John 12:3

What extravagance! What love! What devotion!
What a waste!

The disciples were shocked. Especially Judas.
"Why wasn't this perfume sold and the money given to
the poor?" he objected. "It was worth a year's wages."

And Mary did get carried away. No one had ever
done anything like this before. Mary Magdalene had
washed Jesus' feet with her tears (*see* Luke 7), but Mary
had broken open the alabaster jar containing her most
precious ointment and poured all of it on His feet.

It was an act of worship, sheer devotion to her
Master. And why not? He had just recently raised her
brother Lazarus from the dead. What would you have
done? It was the only way for Mary to express her
gratitude. She gave the most expensive thing she had to

the Savior. No holding back, no halfhearted thanks. Mary gave it all.

Mary was known for sitting at Jesus' feet and she was one of His best listeners. She was a devoted follower. She hung on Jesus' every word, for which He commended her (*see* Luke 10:39-42). And on this evening six days before the Passover, she seemed to sense what lay ahead. Perhaps she knew that time was running out.

Mary was also an emotional person. When Lazarus died, she fell at Jesus' feet and sobbed uncontrollably. He was so moved by her tears that He began to weep Himself. Mary is an example to us all of the kind of passionate commitment that moves the heart of God. She sat at Jesus' feet; she fell at Jesus' feet; and now she anoints Jesus' feet.

Mary's deed was worship in action. She did not limit her response nor was she inhibited by the crowd. Jesus and Lazarus were special guests at a dinner at the home of Simon (cf. Matthew 26:6). The disciples were there as well, making at least 15 men. Martha, as usual, served the meal. It was her way of showing her appreciation to Jesus.

The dinner was undoubtedly a joyous and festive occasion. The resurrection of Lazarus was still fresh in everyone's mind. It was a time of celebration and the men rejoiced together as Simon's guests. Laughter filled the room. The Savior had come to dinner, and the house was filled with excitement and activity.

But Mary could not contain herself. She was filled with awe and worship. A sense of God's presence overcame her and her love for Jesus was so great that she was moved to get the alabaster jar full of perfume, make her way toward Him, kneel at His feet, and break the seal. Soon the precious contents began spilling on His feet, which she wiped with her hair.

The perfume (pure oil of spikenard) was so strong that it saturated the room. There was no question about what she had done; everyone could smell it. The group's eyes probably began to water and their noses may have stopped up as the aroma of sweet perfume filled the room.

The whole incident is a beautiful picture of true worship. Mary held back nothing. She bowed herself before her Lord and poured out every last drop in honor of Him. True worship unites us to the very heart of God. It joins us to the heavenly host who worship in His presence continually.

Critics of true worship will always react like Judas. "What a waste! You poured out your life, time, and devotion to someone else. How foolish!"

"Leave her alone," Jesus told the disciples. "It was intended that she should save this perfume for the day of my burial." Mary's action was all in the plan of God. Her worship came just in time—"six days before the Passover," we read in John 12:1.

Had Mary waited any longer, she would have missed her opportunity. How many times has God prompted your heart to respond to Him in a certain way? Sometimes it is necessary to drop everything you are doing—even if it means setting this book down for a moment, falling on your face before the Lord, and washing His feet with the rich perfume of worship.

Mary was so filled with adoration and wonder that worship broke forth from her soul. She broke open the jar because God had broken open her heart. The fragrance gushed forth because her heart refused to bottle up her love for the Savior.

Oh, that we could love Him that way! Complete and total devotion. On our faces at His feet, with tears of wonder, joy, and love. With every beat of our hearts beating for Him. With every thought of our minds focused on Him.

A.W. Tozer calls such worship the "gaze of faith" when the inward eyes of man are raised to meet the all-seeing eyes of God.[1] Then he quotes Nicholas of Cusa, who wrote four centuries ago: "All my devotion is turned toward you because all your devotion is turned toward me. I look unto you alone with all my attention... because you have looked toward me alone. And what, Lord, is my life, save that embrace wherein your sweetness so lovingly enfolds me."[2]

True love is true worship, and true worship is true love. We worship Him because we love Him, and we love Him because He *first* loved us. We can't help ourselves! We are drawn irresistibly by His love and we bow before Him and offer our richest praise and adoration.

No one else deserves such love, such praise, such worship. Jesus alone is worthy of it all. Because there is no greater Savior. ✳

# 2
~

# A Servant's Heart

*esus . . . wrapped a towel around his waist. . . . and began to wash his disciples' feet, drying them with the towel that was wrapped around him.*

John 13:3-5

It was Passover, the "Days of Unleavened Bread." The Passover meal had to be prepared—lamb, wine, bread, bitter herbs. All had to be gathered in time for the *seder*.

Passover was the time when the Jewish people celebrated their deliverance from bondage in Egypt. It commemorated the time when the blood of the lamb was applied to the doorposts to protect them from the death angel, who passed over and slayed all the firstborn in Egypt.

Jesus told Peter and John to make preparations for them to eat the Passover meal in an upper room in Jerusalem. He told them they would meet a man carrying a jar of water in the city (see Luke 22:10). "Follow him to the house that he enters," Jesus said.

"He will have a guest room we can use for the Passover meal."

This would be a special Passover for the disciples because it would be their last with the Master. On that unique evening, Jesus would use the Passover to institute the Lord's Supper. Borrowing the elements of bread and wine, He would explain that they symbolized His body and blood which were to be given on their behalf.

Jesus Himself would be the sacrificial lamb and His death would remove the bitter herbs of sin. The symbolism was a perfect picture of what was going to transpire the next day. Little did the disciples realize this would be their last supper together. Before that night was over, everything would be changed—dramatically and forever.

They did not know the significance of the evening, and so they started arguing once again about who was the greatest. It probably began over the seating arrangements. Who is going to be the honored guest? Judas? Well, who gets to sit next to Jesus? John—the youngest? What about Peter? Andrew? Matthew?

Most scholars believe the group sat on the floor, reclining on their sides around a three-sided *triclinium* table, with the food an arm's length away in the middle. This setting was very typical in the first-century A.D. Roman world, even in Jerusalem.

Such an arrangement would have fit the biblical description of Jesus, the host, sitting between Judas and John. Close enough to give Judas the sop and close enough to lean over to talk to John.

Everyone else filled in around the three sides of the table in a "U" shape formation. Peter evidently sat near the far end from where he had a clear view to signal John about the betrayer. He was probably the most disgruntled person there. After all, he had helped John set up the room. And he didn't even get a special seat!

Jesus rebuked the men for behaving like Gentiles and He reminded them that the greatest is the person who serves, not the person who waits to be served. That, in turn, brought up a point of protocol. No one had yet assumed the role of a servant and volunteered to wash the others' feet.

Foot washing—a disgusting job! Only the lowest servants did it. But the servant normally responsible for this chore wasn't there that night. And none of the disciples were about to take on a job done by the lowest of servants. They all thought they were the greatest. So everyone's feet remained unwashed.

Over in the corner, near the door, sat a jar of water and an empty basin. They were untouched. There is no mention of the homeowner nor the servant. They must have gone elsewhere to eat the Passover. Only Jesus and the Twelve are in the Upper Room, alone with the water jar and the empty basin.

After the meal, Jesus arose, took off His robe, and wrapped a towel around His waist. He poured water out of the jar and filled the basin. Then, stooping down, our Lord began to wash the disciples' feet. They were astonished. The Master, serving as foot-washer?

"No," Peter protested, "you shall never wash my feet."

But Jesus did. He washed all their feet. He who had His own feet bathed by Mary's perfume now assumed the posture of the lowest servant among them and washed His disciples' feet. "I have set you an example," Jesus said. "No servant is greater than his master." A bit earlier He also said, "You . . . should wash one another's feet."

Here was the Lord of the universe . . . washing men's feet. The Master was bowing to His servants, doing for them what they were not willing to do for each other.

It was just like Jesus to do this! He was always doing the unexpected, even the unimaginable. That is what made Him great. His greatness was in His Person, not just His power. It was in His passion, not just His performance. It was in His manner, not just His miracles.

Jesus was unique among all religious leaders or teachers. He never demanded worship. People fell before Him because of His greatness. They were overwhelmed by *who* He was as well as *what* He was. They were drawn irresistibly to Him.

The washing of feet symbolized the need for daily cleansing. Jesus told Peter he was already clean—he didn't need a bath. He just needed to remove the dust of the day's journey. In the same way, Jesus has already cleansed us from sin's guilt by His blood, but the repeated daily cleansing is His continued work on our behalf. He reminds us of our daily sins that need to be dealt with by "the washing with water through the word" (Ephesians 5:26).

Have you picked up any dirt today? The first-century world was a dusty place. Feet had to be washed every day. Our own world is a spiritually corrupt and dirty place, too. Every day we see and hear things that defile us and can affect our walk with God.

Take a few moments right now to ask yourself, Have I picked up any dirt today? Do I need to take time to let the Holy Spirit cleanse my mind, heart, and life? Before you rush off to take care of the day's business, take time to draw near to the Savior.

He's waiting. Towel in hand. ✳

# 3

## So Many Questions

*T*homas said to him, *"Lord, we don't
know where you are going, so how can
we know the way?" Jesus answered, "I
am the way and the truth and the life."*

John 14:5-6

Questions . . . so many questions. The disciples'
minds were spinning. Is He actually going to wash our
feet? Who is going to betray Him? Where is He going?
When? Why? How?

As the Last Supper proceeded, the disciples were
amazed again and again. They had sensed the tension in
Jerusalem. They knew they were there at great risk and
heard Jesus warn that the end was coming. But no one
expected this!

John 13–14 records seven questions Jesus'
disciples asked Him in the Upper Room. The discourse
that follows was given in response to those questions. In
each case our Lord gave words of hope and encouragement to the disciples. As we examine His answers, we,
too, can find hope and encouragement.

1. *Peter: "Lord, are you going to wash my feet?" (13:6).*

When Jesus attempted to wash Peter's feet, the disciple objected. But Jesus reminded Peter that unless He did, Peter would have no fellowship with Him.

"Then, Lord . . . not just my feet but my hands and my head as well!" Peter insisted.

But that wasn't necessary. Those who have already had a bath need only their feet washed. Likewise, we who are saved have already been bathed in the blood of Christ, and now we merely need the daily cleansing that foot washing symbolizes.

2. *John: "Lord, who is it?" (13:25).*

As the disciples sat down around the table, Jesus stunned them again. "One of you is going to betray Me," He said.

Peter motioned across the table to John. "Ask Him which one He means," he directed. John was sitting next to Jesus, so he leaned back and asked, "Lord, who is it?"

"The one to whom I will give this piece of bread," the Lord replied. Then He dipped it and handed it to Judas.

What a dreadful moment that must have been. Once Judas took the bread and left the table, it was all over. He had made a series of choices from which there would be no retreat. Any chance for repentance was over. Judas was determined to carry out his deed and he disappeared into the darkness of the night—forever lost.

Many of us come to a moment of decision like that. Everything is at stake. The decision we make at that point will determine our fate and our future. It will enable us to go on with God or it will hinder our walk with Him. Nothing will ever be the same again. For Judas, it was the beginning of the end.

3. *Peter: "Lord, where are you going?"* (13:36).

As soon as Judas left the room, Jesus announced His own departure. "Now is the Son of Man glorified," He said. Glorified? How? By His death on the cross—an event put into motion by Judas' betrayal. The wheels of divine justice were moving toward the climax of history, and Jesus knew it.

"Where I am going, you cannot come," Jesus explained.

"Lord, where are you going?" Peter asked.

"You cannot follow now, but you will follow later," Jesus explained.

There are some things we just aren't ready for right now, and our Lord knows it. He sees the end from the beginning. Heaven could wait for the disciples, but not for Jesus. The time had come to go home.

4. *Peter: "Lord, why can't I follow you now?"* (13:37).

Separation was the last thing on the disciples' minds. He's leaving us? No, not now! Why can't we come?

"I will lay down my life for you," Peter protested. He was insisting that he was ready to go anywhere that his Lord needed him.

"Will you really lay down your life for me?" Jesus asked Peter. "I tell you the truth, before the rooster crows, you will disown me three times!"

Peter denied it would happen, but it did. Three times, just as Jesus had predicted.

How many times have we made a similar protest? "Lord, I'll stand for you! I'll do what's right!" Only to fall flat on our faces. Self-confidence is often a prelude to failure. The more convinced we are that we can handle things on our own, the more likely we are to make a mess of them.

5. *Thomas: "How can we know the way?" (14:5).*

After Jesus announced His departure to His disciples, He told them He was going to His Father's house to prepare a place for them. He promised to come again to take them to that place. "You know the way to the place where I am going," Jesus said, speaking of heaven.

"Lord, we don't know where you are going," Thomas protested. "So how can we know the way?"

The answer to Thomas' question was one of Jesus' most powerful pronouncements. In response to the disciples' discouragement and frustration, the Lord proclaimed, "I am the way and the truth and the life."

In that magnificent threefold declaration is an incredible depth of divine truth. Jesus announces that He is the way to heaven, He is the truth of God, and He is the very life of the Almighty. No declaration of one's personhood could be more conclusive. Jesus is divine, the link between God and man.

Fortunately, He does not merely claim to be the *way*—follow Me. Or even the *truth*—believe Me. But He also declares that He is the very *life* of God—let Me live through you.

If Jesus did not promise us eternal life, we would still be without hope. Without Him, we are *lost* and cannot find the way. We are *blind* and cannot see the truth. We are *dead* and cannot live the life. Therefore, He must impart His life to us in order for us to see the truth and follow the right way.

6. *Philip: "Lord, show us the Father" (14:8).*

Jesus turned Philip's request into a question. "How can you say, 'Show us the Father?' Anyone who has seen me has seen the Father."

If the disciples had not yet understood Jesus' claim to be divine, this should have clinched it. To see Christ in the flesh is to see God incarnate. The Father is a spirit, thus, as the Bible says, no one has ever seen God. The only member of the Godhead to appear in human form is the Son.

"I am in the Father," Jesus explained, "and the Father is in me" (14:10). They are inseparable. To believe in one is to believe in the other. To know one is to know the other.

If you know Jesus as your personal Savior, you know the Father. If Christ lives within your heart, so does the Father. To have one is to have the other. When you were born again, God came to live within you. Your life was reborn and you became co-eternal with God. You will live as long as God lives because God lives in you.

7. *Judas (Thaddeus): "Lord, why do you intend to show yourself to us and not to the world?" (14:22)*

Jesus had explained that in His departure to heaven, He would show Himself unto His own. How? Why?

The answer was simple but profound. "We will come to him," Jesus said, "and make our home with him" (14:23). How would the Father and the Son do that? By sending the Holy Spirit to indwell the believer's heart. The Counselor would come to live within believers and seal their lives to the life of God.

What a powerful truth! God Himself lives within you because His Spirit dwells within you. In the Old Testament era, God dwelled only in the Temple, inside the Holy of Holies. But from now on, Jesus promised, He would dwell in *us*. We ourselves are now the Temple of God.

On that last evening together in the Upper Room, Jesus answered the concerns of His disciples. And today, He cares for us in the same way. Whatever your struggles may be, bring them to Jesus. He can answer every one and meet every need. He is the same Savior today as He was then. Bring your questions to Him. And He will give you the personal attention you need . . . right now. ✳

# 4

~

# Your Own Personal
# Counselor

*U*nless I go away, the Counselor will not
come to you; but if I go, I will send
him to you.

                                                                    John 16:7

Have you ever felt as if you could use a good
counselor? The disciples certainly felt that way in John
13–14! Jesus had just explained that He would be leaving
them and returning to heaven. They were stunned,
upset, dismayed. How were they going to go on without
Jesus?

Our Lord gave them the reassurance they
needed. He would send the Holy Spirit in His place—
the Counselor (Greek, *paraclete*, which means "advocate"
or "comforter"). In His farewell address, Jesus referred to
the Spirit seven times: four times as the "Counselor"
(14:16; 14:26; 15:26; 16:7) and three times as the "Spirit
of truth" (14:17; 15:26; 16:13).

The Holy Spirit would come in Jesus' place to
indwell all believers. He would become the permanent
spiritual link to the Father. His presence in their lives

would seal them to Him forever and He would reside within their hearts and transform their lives.

The Spirit would also perform a special ministry in relation to the world. He would convince men of their need for the Savior and point men to Jesus as the only one who could meet their needs. He would not come to call attention to Himself, but to the Son.

The Holy Spirit's ministry to unbelievers would convince them of their need for salvation. He and He alone would bring men and women to the point where they would consider the claims of Christ upon their lives. Think of how He worked in your life, convicting you of sin and convincing you of the payment for that sin in Jesus Christ.

The Spirit's ministry to unbelievers includes three aspects: He *convicts of sin*, in which He alone convicts us that we are sinners; He *convinces of righteousness*, in which He leads us to Christ's righteousness, which makes us acceptable to God; and He *confirms a time of judgment*, in which He testifies that sin has been judged by Christ's victorious death.

Eventually we all have to come face to face with the claims of Christ, but it is the Holy Spirit who must convince us of those claims. We dare not assume that we can casually come to God on our own terms, whenever we decide the time is convenient. The Holy Spirit must convict, convince, and compel us to come. He alone is the agent of God's grace which draws us to the Savior.

The Spirit regenerates our hearts, indwells our lives, fills our souls, empowers our service, and seals us to the life of God for all eternity. He brings the very life of God into the heart of every believer.

The Spirit's ministry to the believer is also described in a threefold manner: He *illuminates the truth* by guiding our understanding of God's Word; He *predicts the future* by revealing the coming of Christ; and He *glorifies Christ* by directing all worship to the Father and the Son.

As Jesus spoke of the Spirit's ministry to the church, He made one thing very clear: The Holy Spirit will not come to call attention to Himself. He will come only to glorify the Lord. The greatest evidence today of the Spirit's presence among us is the glorification of Jesus Christ.

Just as John the Baptist pointed the way to Christ, so also does the Holy Spirit point us to Christ. He actively invades our lives, draws us to the Savior, seals us to God, and perpetuates and empowers our spiritual service for all eternity.

Don't be guilty of thinking you can live the Christian life without God. Unless He lives in us and through us, we are living in vain. Unless He empowers us, we have no power. Unless He sustains us, we have no hope.

Ask yourself: Where would I be today without God? What if Jesus had never lived? What if the Holy Spirit had never come? How would I face the future? How would I face today?

Dr. James Kennedy has written: "If Christ had not come, life would be meaningless. . . . If Christ had not come, there would be no forgiveness of sin. If Christ had not come, there would be no true freedom from guilt."[3] Lives of countless millions would never have been changed. Mankind would be left without hope, awash in its own vices, lost in its own sinfulness, engulfed in its own hopelessness.

The Holy Spirit serves as our permanently indwelling Counselor. He will not leave us nor forsake us. In our Savior's earthly absence, He fills our hearts with God's presence.

During His farewell address, Jesus used the phrase "a little while" seven times (John 16:16-19). He wanted the disciples to understand that His initial absence would be brief. "You will grieve," He said, "but your grief will turn to joy" (John 16:20). The resurrection would reverse their sorrow.

But then a greater and longer separation was to follow. Christ would return to heaven and the disciples would have to carry on without Him. How? By the indwelling presence of the Holy Spirit. Jesus explained it like this: "We will come to him and make our home with him" (John 14:23).

Isn't that amazing? God lives within you. He has chosen to take up residence in your soul. This Spirit is alive within you. He is your own personal Counselor. His wisdom, guidance, and strength are yours. He will lead, guide, and instruct you.

What are you waiting for? Ask your questions. Seek His advice. You don't even need to schedule an appointment. He is on call anytime, day or night. He is ready to hear you and willing to help you. All you have to do is ask. ✳

# 5

## Someone Is Praying for You

*I am not praying for the world, but for those you have given me. . . . I pray also for those who will believe in me through their message.*

John 17:9,20

Have you ever wished someone were praying for you? That someone could truly understand what you were going through? And that you could count on him to bring your name and your needs to the Father?

Most of us go through times like that—times when we wish there were someone *special* to turn to with our problems. Times when we just can't go on alone. Times when we need to know someone else cares, that someone else is there, praying for us and with us.

The Bible reveals that such special help and prayer *is* available to us. John 17 tells us that Jesus is praying for us personally and individually. This chapter provides a remarkable glimpse into the prayer life of our Lord. Jesus' prayer in John 17 has been called "the High Priestly Prayer" because it is a prayer of intercession on our behalf.

Consider the setting of this prayer. The Lord Jesus
has already announced His soon departure. He has
reassured the disciples that the Holy Spirit will be with
them in the meantime. Then, as they all prepare to
leave the Upper Room and make their way to Gethsemane, Jesus begins to pray. And what a prayer it was!

This prayer may appropriately be called "the Lord's
Prayer." It reflects the thoughts that were upon His
mind as He took those final steps that lead to Calvary.
Truly, while He was on the cross, we were on His mind.

As you read this prayer in John 17, look for the
shadow of the cross. It falls across every line and
touches every word and phrase. Jesus was on His way to
Gethsemane and from there to Golgotha. All that time,
we were on His heart.

John chapter 17 has also been called "the Holy of
Holies" of the New Testament. Here we see revealed a
Savior who truly loves us, One who is willing to die for
us.

The prayer opens with our Lord crying out to the
Father. He has finished His earthly ministry and it is
time to go home.

"Father, the time has come. Glorify your Son,
that your Son may glorify you." As Jesus faces the cross,
He anticipates its victory. It will be His crowning
achievement and it will signal His final triumph.

Donald Carson has observed, "Both aspects
contribute to Jesus' glory. Jesus prays for glory, both
the glory connected with the cross and the glory
connected with the exaltation."4 To the Romans, the
cross was a symbol of shame and evil. But to Jesus, it
was a symbol of God's redeeming love. It was the visible
demonstration of God's saving grace on our behalf.

The Savior had understood this all along. That is
why He had often remarked, "The Son of Man must be

lifted up, that everyone who believes in him may have eternal life" (John 3:14-15). He foresaw the cross. He knew that being "lifted up" meant crucifixion—but He also knew it meant triumph, victory, and glory!

The heart of our Lord's prayer in John 17 focuses on His disciples (verses 6-19). The Savior refers to them as "those whom you [the Father] gave me out of the world." Most of us think of Jesus as God's gift to us. We rarely consider ourselves as God's gift to Jesus. But we are.

"They were yours," Jesus proclaims, "you gave them to me."

We are God's gifts to His Son. What a thought! But who would want us? What kind of gift are we? We are trophies of His grace, the evidence of His triumph.

A thousand years earlier, the psalmist recorded these words:

> You are my Son,
>    today I have become your Father.
> Ask of me,
>    and I will make the nations your inheritance,
>    the ends of the earth your possession
>    (Psalm 2:7-8).

The Father promised to give us to the Son, and Jesus was ready to claim His inheritance. He had come to earth to redeem the sons of men. He had come to gather the elect of the Father. He had come to claim His own.

"I pray for them," Jesus said boldly. "I am not praying for the world, but for those you have given me" (verse 9). Here is the *great division* in this prayer. As Jesus faces the cross the next morning, He makes it clear that He has only one category of people on His heart— those who will believe.

The unbeliever has no place in this prayer. He cannot and will not benefit from the Savior's prayer because he will not accept His provision or receive His blessings or partake of His salvation.

Jesus prays that God will preserve His disciples in this world. "My prayer is not that you take them out of the world but that you protect them from the evil one" (verse 15).

It is not our Lord's plan to save us and then remove us from the world. His ultimate purpose is to leave us as a witness to the world. Leaving us here to do His work is just as important as taking us to heaven to be with Him.

The final portion of this prayer (verses 20-26) is where we come in. Here, our Lord said, "My prayer is not for them alone. I pray also for those who will believe in me through their message, that all of them may be one."

As Jesus looked toward the agony of Gethsemane and as He considered the humiliation of betrayal, arrest, and denial—as He faced the horror of the cross—one thing kept Him focused. One thing propelled Him. One thing determined that He keep this date with destiny— *you!*

He did it for you! He went to the cross for you. He suffered the agony and the pain for you. He bore the sins of the world for you. Even as He made His way to Gethsemane, He was praying for you.

Jesus saw beyond the 12 disciples. He saw the multiplied millions who would come to believe in Him. And in that moment He prayed for all of us. He prayed for you.

Is someone praying for you today? Yes! Jesus is praying for you. He has been praying for you ever since He went to the cross to pay for your sins. And He is still praying for you today.

The Bible reminds us, "Therefore, since we have a great high priest who has gone through the heavens, Jesus the Son of God. . . . Let us then approach the throne of grace with confidence, so that we may receive mercy and find grace to help us in our time of need" (Hebrews 4:14-16).

Take time right now to open your heart to Him. Unload your burdens. Share your hurts. Jesus is *always* willing to listen. Are you willing to pray? ✳

# 6

## If Olive Trees Could Weep

*O*n the other side there was an olive grove.
. . . Now Judas, who betrayed him, knew
the place, because Jesus had often met
there with his disciples.

John 18:1-2

The olive trees have been there for centuries.
They were old even in Jesus' time. Huge, gnarled trunks,
scrawny leaves, spring flowers popping up here and
there. It is still a beautiful and peaceful spot today.

No wonder they came there often—the serene
setting, the gorgeous scenery, the spectacular view. You
can sit in Gethsemane, on the lower slopes of the
Mount of Olives, and look across the Kidron Valley
toward Jerusalem. There in the distance is the Eastern
Gate (or the Golden Gate, as some call it). This is the
gate through which the prophets predicted the Messiah
would come to claim the throne of David.

How often the disciples must have gathered
there, walking with the King, talking about the
kingdom, and looking forward to His ultimate triumph.
This was their favorite spot. From here they could

imagine how it would be—Jesus marching in triumph with the disciples at His side.

These had been incredible times. If the olive trees could have listened, they would have heard the disciples' expressions of joy and confidence—their hopes, their dreams, their plans, and their goals. It had all been discussed so many times before, right there in the olive garden.

Little did the disciples realize that one day, this beautiful place would become the setting for ugly deeds. Here, one of them would betray Him, another would be rebuked by Him, and all of them would forsake Him.

Here in this beautiful spot, the wheels of human depravity would begin to move. Satan would call the shots, devise the plan, and provoke his pawns to do his will. Here in a garden he would try again to thwart the plan of God.

Satan was used to garden settings. He seems to be at his best when he is camouflaged by God's creative masterpieces. For it was in another garden, at Eden, that he had pulled off his great (but temporary) victory.

There he captured Adam and Eve in the sin that condemned the human race. Cleverly disguised, the father of lies, the master of deception, had taken them unawares. Now he would try it again.

The contrast between Eden and Gethsemane is the Tale of Two Gardens. In the one, paradise was lost; in the other, paradise was regained. In the one, Satan triumphed; in the other, God was the victor. In the one, mankind was lost; in the other, mankind was redeemed. In the one, God's will was violated; in the other, God's will was vindicated.

Jesus and the disciples arrived in the middle of the night. It was dark and no one saw them enter the garden, but Judas knew the place well. He had been there many times before and he guessed that was where they would go to spend the night after the Passover meal in the Upper Room.

He came with a "detachment of soldiers"—the Temple guards, authorized by the high priest. Why he did this, we can only speculate.

Perhaps he was afraid the end was coming and he wanted to protect himself. Maybe he was jealous or bitter or scared. Perhaps he thought Jesus was going too far and needed to be stopped (for His own good, of course).

Whatever his reasoning, Judas made his pact with the enemy for 30 pieces of silver, the price of a common slave. Thirty pieces of silver that changed the course of history.

Humanly speaking, everything went wrong that night. The disciples fell asleep. The Savior was left to pray alone. Peter overreacted. Jesus rebuked him. The disciples fled. And the Lord of glory was arrested and taken to a trial that was illegitimate because it was held in the middle of the night.

Things could not have gone worse. The Creator had been arrested by His own creatures. If olive trees could weep, they would have sobbed that night. What injustice! What inhumanity! What indecency!

"Don't take Him away!" They would have shouted. "Don't remove the One who has blessed the garden so often by His presence. Bring Him back!" They wanted to cry, "He is the Lord. The Savior. The King!"

But no one heard the trees that night. In fact, no one was hearing much of anything. For instance, Jesus asked Judas, "Friend, why have you come?" (Matthew 26:50). His question must have cut through Judas's heart. Judas had one last opportunity to repent, but he didn't.

"Who is it you want?" Jesus asked the guards.

"Jesus of Nazareth," they replied.

"I am He," Jesus announced boldly.

Three times He said it; the first time they fell to the ground helpless. They could have returned without Him, but they didn't.

Then Peter pulled out his sword. "I'll protect you," he may have said. He swung at the high priest's servant—a safer target than an armed soldier—and cut off his ear.

"Put your sword away!" Jesus told him. Our Lord could have called the angels to deliver Him, but He didn't.

*How could God let this happen?* Have you ever asked yourself that question? Not only about Jesus but about yourself? God, how could you let this happen to me? Where were you when I needed you?

Sometimes there is a silence in God's providence. We listen for His voice, but hear nothing. We seek His face, but see nothing.

So it was that night. Even as Jesus replaced the servant's ear, the soldiers bound His hands and led Him away. His last miracle took place in the olive garden.

And the trees watched—if trees can watch. Judas went off to collect his reward, the disciples ran to escape into the darkness of the night, and the soldiers led the Savior away to the palace of the high priest.

The garden was empty now. The night was dark. The breeze was cool. And dew drops formed on the olive leaves—the tears of God.

If olive trees could weep, they wept that night. Not for Jesus, for it was the hour of His triumph. But for those who came so close, and yet missed so much. ✳

# 7

# Too Close to
# the Fire

*idn't I see you with him in the olive grove?" Again Peter denied it, and at that moment a rooster began to crow.*

John 18:26-27

They should have run off like the others, but Peter and John followed Jesus and the guards to the high priest's palace. To be sure, they stayed back at a safe distance. But there they were, tagging along, wondering what would happen next.

The courtyard gate was locked by the time they arrived. The guards ushered Jesus inside and the gate was closed. But John knew the gatekeeper.

"Please let us in," he may have pleaded. "We'll stand quietly in the back."

Scholars believe the open courtyard was surrounded by a stone wall. At one end stood the mansion of the high priest. Homes of this magnitude usually had a second-story balcony overlooking the courtyard. There, Jesus would be brought before selected members of the Sanhedrin.

It wasn't an official trial. In fact, it wasn't even legal to conduct such an inquisition at night. But they did it anyway. Jesus stood on the balcony facing His accusers, with His back to the audience in the courtyard below.

Over in one corner some servants had built a fire to warm themselves from the chilly night air. John disappeared into the crowd, and Peter eventually made his way over to the fire.

At some point the people standing around the fire began talking about the prisoner and the trial. Peter probably hovered in silence over the fire; this was one discussion he didn't plan to enter. *Silence, that's it. I'll just stand here quietly, listening to the rest of them.* But they wouldn't let him. Besides, he looked different and he spoke with a Galilean accent.

Who was this stranger? Why was he here by the fire? Then a servant girl recognized him.

"Weren't you also with Jesus of Galilee?" she asked.

"I don't know what you're talking about," Peter replied (Matthew 26:70).

*That's not really a denial*, Peter may have thought. *Just play dumb, that's all. Tell them you don't know anything about all this.*

How many times have we done the same thing? Someone innocently pressed us about our Christian commitment, and we acted like we had no idea what they were talking about.

The accusation must have made Peter nervous. Matthew's account indicates he moved toward the gate, perhaps intending to leave (26:71). But then another girl recognized him. "This fellow was with Jesus of Nazareth," she announced to those nearby.

This time Peter's denial was more forceful. He swore with an oath that he did not know Jesus.

"I swear to God."

That's always a dead giveaway that somebody is lying. There is just something about human nature that compels people to say that when they're desperate. And Peter was desperate.

He was trapped. The girl at the fire had embarrassed him, and now a girl by the gate had pointed him out. There wasn't anywhere to go, so he made his way back to the fire.

But again there was no relief. Someone picked up on his Galilean accent. It stood out among all the Judean voices.

"Surely you are one of them, for your accent gives you away," they began to say.

Then someone else in the group recognized Peter. It was a relative of the man whose ear Peter had cut off. "Didn't I see you with him in the olive grove?" he asked.

At that moment, Peter panicked. He lost all composure, as guilty people often do. And he blew up. Matthew tells us he began to curse and swear and violently deny that he ever knew Jesus (26:74).

It is hard to imagine one of Jesus' disciples reacting the way Peter did. In a fit of rage, he began to curse like an unbeliever. And it worked—for a moment, anyway.

Whenever we act like unbelievers, people treat us like unbelievers. It is the ultimate spiritual compromise. Incognito Christianity works every time. It's like going underground. We become God's "secret agents," stealthing around unidentified. We never reveal our true identity unless we see another believer; the rest of the world treats us like we are one of them. And why not? For in those moments of spiritual compromise, we *are* one of them!

At that moment the rooster began crowing—*in the middle of the night.* It was most unexpected, but it was just as Jesus had predicted at the Last Supper.

Luke 22:61 tells us that at that moment, Jesus turned His back on the members of the Sanhedrin. He looked out over the crowd in the courtyard below and His eyes fell on Peter.

Their eyes met. That was all it took. "Then Peter remembered," Luke tells us. In that one momentary glance from the Savior, Peter came face to face with himself, his arrogance, and his cowardice.

Luke does not describe the Savior's look. We can only imagine it must have been the look of a broken heart. But certainly it was also a look of love and compassion. *I still love you! I am still willing to go to the cross for you and everyone else like you. I will do for you what you cannot do for yourself. I will give you what you do not deserve.*

We cannot fully comprehend such love. God's love is so incredible that He turns our worst mistakes into the greatest displays of His grace. If we had been in Jesus' place, we would have condemned Peter's disloyalty, made an example of his failure, and condemned him to hell. We certainly would not have gone to the cross the next day to die for the likes of him.

But that is why we are what we are—sinners. And that is why He is what He is—the Savior.

Then, Jesus did the unthinkable. The unimaginable. The incredible. He went ahead and marched right up to the cross. He took all our denials, all our failures, all our sin, and nailed it all to the cross.

And said, "It is finished." ✳

# 8
~

# A Tale of
# Two Choices

*W*hen Judas, who had betrayed him,
saw that Jesus was condemned, he . . .
threw the money into the temple and
left. Then he went away and hanged himself.

Matthew 27:3,5

Judas Iscariot was the only Judean among the
disciples, yet he had a place of honor. He was their
treasurer. He was probably interested in money to begin
with, a sort of detailed person who liked to keep receipts
and hold down expenditures.

But Judas was also a victim of money. He was
addicted to greed. He got upset when Mary broke the
alabaster vase and poured out the expensive perfume on
Jesus' feet.

"Why wasn't this perfume sold and the money
given to the poor?" he objected.

But the Bible explains that Judas didn't care
about the poor as much as he cared about himself. He
liked controlling the purse because he liked being able
to help himself from time to time (*see* John 12:6). So

accepting the 30 pieces of silver fell right in line with his character weakness.

Greedy people are usually insecure people, and *things* make them feel better about themselves. The more they have, the happier they are, and the more willing they are to sacrifice the well-being of others for their own personal gain.

We have no way of knowing what prompted Judas to go to the Temple leaders in the first place. Whatever the reason, the Bible makes it clear that Judas did not anticipate Jesus being handed over to the Romans to be executed. Like most shortsighted people, he hadn't fully considered the consequences of his actions.

We all think of Judas as a bad guy—that's because of how his story ends. He was upset and filled with remorse. He even took the money back and threw it down. But then he went out and killed himself. The whole nasty escapade ended in self-destruction.

By contrast, we remember Peter as a good guy—despite his three denials. What's the difference? Weren't the denials as bad as the betrayal? Certainly! But the difference is in how the story ends. Peter repented and was restored. Judas didn't and wasn't.

Here is a Tale of Two Disciples, Judas and Peter. Both were followers of Christ. Both had committed their lives to the Master. Both were associated with Him in His ministry and His miracles. But one was a phony; the other, a traitor. One rejected God's conviction in his life; the other refused to repent.

Jesus called Judas "the son of perdition" (John 17:12 KJV). He was the one "doomed to destruction" (NIV). Despite being in Jesus' presence for three years, Judas ended his life by turning away from the Savior.

How could Judas have been so close to Jesus and

yet not become changed? How could he go out and hang himself?

Desperate people do desperate things, and guilty people do destructive things. Whenever you wed guilt to desperation, the result will always be self-destruction. By hanging himself, Judas said no to God one last, decisive time.

His suicide was his final act of rebellion, his final moment of resistance to God's will for his life. When he said no this time, it was forever.

Peter, on the other hand, was also crushed by the consequences of his sin. But instead of destroying an opportunity for reconciliation, he created one. Faced with his denials, the Bible says, Peter rushed out of the courtyard and "wept bitterly" (Matthew 26:75).

Peter's tears were not merely tears of anguish. They were tears of repentance. His heart was broken. But in the *breaking* of Peter was the *making* of Peter. He would never again be so filled with pride and arrogance as to vault himself above the others. Out of his brokenness, a new and humbler servant of God would emerge.

No person likes to go through brokenness. It hurts so much. It tears away at every fiber of our humanness and reduces us to the lowest possible level of our existence. It leaves us battered and dazed with no confidence in ourselves.

Broken people, however, are candidates for God's divine repair shop. The Savior reaches out to us to help put the pieces of our lives back together. He loves us when no one else loves us, sees our potential when no one else sees it.

God never gives up on us unless we give up on ourselves. That's what happened to Judas. He gave up. In total desperation, he may have assumed that his failure was beyond forgiveness, his greed beyond grace, his larceny beyond love.

Judas underestimated the grace of God. A God who could forgive Peter could have forgiven Judas. A God whose grace was sufficient for Peter would have been sufficient for Judas. But Judas said, "No!"

Every time we walk away from God, we walk away from His grace. Our salvation does not depend on our behavior; it depends on His grace. Our spiritual growth does not rely on our efforts, but on His great love for us.

The key is in *how* we respond to our troubles. We will all fail at times. We will all make mistakes and live with regrets. But we need not let those mistakes destroy us.

If you are struggling today with failure in your life, even serious failure, remember Peter and Judas. One handled his failure the right way; the other did not. One found repentance, restitution, and reinstatement; the other closed his eyes to God, to life, and to hope.

Turn around before it's too late. The last chapter of your life doesn't have to be written with the pen of regret. It can be rewritten with the indelible ink of God's grace. ✳

# 9

# What's the
# Big Idea?

*S*o Pilate came out to them and asked,
*"What charges are you bringing against
this man?"*

John 18:29

It was very early in the morning when the Jewish
religious leaders got Pilate out of bed—not usually a
good idea when dealing with Roman governors. But the
Jewish leaders were desperate.

They wanted Jesus executed for blasphemy, but
they didn't have the authority to do it themselves. They
needed official sanction from the Roman government.
And they were in luck. The governor himself, Pontias
Pilate, was in town for the Passover festivities.

When the little inquisition at the high priest's
house had ended, they tore their robes and shouted
"Blasphemy!" They even hit Jesus in the face and spat
on Him in contempt.

"He is worthy of death," they shouted.

Then the fateful decision was made. Take Him
first thing in the morning to Pilate. Early. Real early. At
six o'clock, before the rest of the city is awake. Accuse

Him of claiming to be a king, of opposing Caesar. Make Him look like a zealot, a revolutionary, a terrorist.

When the Jewish leaders arrive at the Roman fortress where Pilate is staying, they knock on the doors and demand justice. The blasphemer must die!

Because the religious leaders did not want to "defile" themselves by entering a Gentile building shortly before Passover, Pilate has to go to the entry gate to speak with them.

"What charges are you bringing against this man?" Pilate demands.

"If he were not a criminal, we would not have handed him over to you," they respond.

"Take him yourselves," Pilate says, "and judge him by your own law."

But they didn't want to do that. They wanted Pilate to judge Him and to authorize His execution.

Finally, under pressure to appease the Jews, Pilate took Jesus into the fortress to question Him. The interaction between Pilate and Jesus is the most classic dialogue of all time: the nervous governor trying to talk his way out of this act of injustice, the priests insisting upon His death, and Jesus rising above it all with superior intelligence, dignity, and character.

What begins as Jesus' trial before Pilate quickly becomes Pilate's trial before Jesus. The governor's vacillation is no match for the Savior's vindication. Pilate's character is no match for Jesus' consistency. His human weakness cannot compare to Jesus' divine strength.

Pilate had never dealt with a man like this. "Let Him go," his wife warned. But he didn't listen. He felt trapped by the whole situation, stuck in the middle. Futilely he tried to balance the Roman sense of justice with the Jewish leaders' demand for action.

In the apostle John's account of the trial, we read of seven questions from Pilate. These form the basis of the governor's interrogation of Jesus. Three times Pilate returns to announce, "I find no fault in him" (18:38; 19:4; 19:6 KJV). But each time he is countered by the Jews, who insist the blasphemer must die.

One cannot read this account without being impressed with Jesus. His responses to Pilate's questions are truly amazing.

### 1. *"Are you the king of the Jews?"* (18:33).

Pilate got right to the point. He was no expert in Jewish theology and he didn't care about charges of heresy. But a usurper—that was a different story. The only problem was that Jesus didn't look like a king.

Jesus answered Pilate's question with a question. "Is that your own idea, or did others talk to you about me?"

### 2. *"Do you think I am a Jew?"* (18:35).

Pilate's implication was this: "I'm not Jewish! Why should I even care? It's Your people and Your chief priests who handed You over to me."

Pilate was saying this is a *Jewish* problem. "You people created this problem. Don't ask me about it. Of course someone else told me this. Someone *Jewish*, like You!"

The animosity between the Jews and the Romans is well attested in ancient historical sources, and Pilate expresses it here. But as the interview unfolds, Pilate begins to express his anger toward Jesus' accusers rather than to Jesus Himself.

### 3. *"What is it you have done?"* (18:35).

The Romans prided themselves on the principle of justice. Though there were bribes, corruption, and political intrigues throughout the empire, justice was still upheld as the ideal. So Pilate attempts to isolate the problem: "Why have they brought You here? What have You done that could possibly be deserving of death?"

Jesus' response made it clear that He was no zealot or revolutionary in the politico-military mold. "My kingdom is not of this world," the Savior announced. "If it were, my servants would fight."

You don't need to defend Jesus; He is fully capable of defending Himself. Yet Jesus' plans for building His spiritual kingdom did not include the use of physical force. Armed resistance is no substitute for spiritual power.

4. *"So you are a king?"* (18:37 NASB).

Pilate's fourth question focuses on the main issue of the accusation: Is Jesus a self-proclaimed king, an insurrectionist, a zealot, a troublemaker?

"You are right in saying I am a king," Jesus replied. "In fact, for this reason I was born, and for this I came into the world, to testify to the truth. Everyone on the side of truth listens to me."

That was a strong statement to make to a Roman official. Roman scholars had struggled for centuries with the issue of truth. And prefects, like Pilate, were supposed to discern the truth before rendering their judgments. But it was at this very point that Pilate began to admit his own uncertainty.

5. *"What is truth?"* (18:38).

Pilate asked the question and left it unanswered. It was a pensive question, a searching question for which the governor had no answer. It was the pivotal point in the interrogation. Pilate knew that pursuing any course of punishment would be unjust. He turned and left abruptly.

"I find no fault in him," Pilate announced. And before the morning was over, he would repeat that two more times. It is recorded not only as the verdict of the Roman governor, but also as the verdict of history itself. It still echoes down the corridor of time: No fault! No fault! No fault!

He in whom there was no fault took upon Himself all our faults. He who knew no sin became sin for us. The guiltless became the guilty so that the guilty may become the guiltless. The righteous became unrighteous so that the unrighteous might become righteous.

Pilate did everything he could to get out of the whole unpleasant matter. He suggested releasing Jesus as a Passover "present." But the crowd refused. Then Pilate had Jesus flogged, hoping that a little blood would pacify them. But they only wanted more.

"He must die," they shouted, "because he claimed to be the Son of God."

Upon hearing this, Pilate returned to the judgment hall. *The Son of God! This was a new twist. Who could I be dealing with?*

6. *"Where do you come from?"* (19:8).

Pilate's question was prompted by fear. Perhaps he had done the wrong thing by flogging this "Son of God." But Jesus, bleeding profusely from the whipping, stood silent. His body was in tatters, but His spirit still stood strong. Pilate waited for an answer, but got none.

7. *"Don't you realize I have power either to free you or to crucify you?"* (19:10).

Pilate was shocked: "You refuse to speak to *me?* Don't You realize who I am?" But it was Jesus who should have asked that question of Pilate. The governor was now talking to Jesus face to face, and yet he never realized the significance of who Jesus was.

Oh, Pilate tried to let Jesus go. But in the end, Pilate caved in to the pressure; his career was at stake. Finally, he gave the order for Jesus to be crucified. Imagine what has gone through Pilate's mind all these centuries as he awaits the coming day of judgment when he will face Jesus again—this time, with their roles reversed.

That day of judgment is coming for us as well. We, too, must stand before the Judge and give an account for what we have done with Him.

Are you ready? ✳

# 10
~

# Let the
# Hammers Ring!

*Carrying his own cross, he went out to The
Place of the Skull. . . . Here they crucified
him, and with him two others—one on each
side and Jesus in the middle.*

John 19:17-18

Crucifixion was a dirty business, and the
Romans were experts at it. They did it all the time.
It was their way of keeping the general public in
submission. Still, it wasn't for everybody; they reserved
this most cruel punishment only for slaves and for-
eigners. Roman citizens were exempt.

Dying on a cross was the worst thing that could
happen to a Jew because such a punishment was
associated with the *curse* of God (*see* Deuteronomy
21:22-23). It was the ultimate humiliation. You were
stripped of your clothes, battered by soldiers, nailed to
the cross bars and hung naked, suspended between
heaven and earth. It was a spectacle of blood, sweat,
and tears!

The condemned man was usually scourged or
flogged. So severe was this beating—administered with

a whip laced with bits of glass or metal—that it could kill a man. It is likely that Jesus' back had already been ripped open like raw meat before He ever went to the cross.

In addition, the Savior had been beaten and mocked. The crown of thorns was jammed on His brow, and He had to carry the cross on His back. Soldiers prodded and beat Him as He staggered through the streets of Jerusalem. The *Via Dolorosa*—the "Way of Sorrows"—was lined with friends, foes, and strangers alike, all clamoring to see Him.

John was the only disciple there, accompanied by Mary, Jesus' mother, her sister Salome, Mary Magdalene, and some women from Galilee. Peter, in his shame, was nowhere to be seen. People wept openly as the procession moved through the streets. Others shouted and cursed. Still others turned away their faces from the awful spectacle.

The prophet Isaiah had predicted it all so clearly. Under divine inspiration, he wrote centuries before:

> There were many who were appalled at him—his appearance was so disfigured beyond that of any man and his form marred beyond human likeness. . . .
> He was despised and rejected by men, a man of sorrows, and familiar with suffering. Like one from whom men hide their faces he was despised, and we esteemed him not (Isaiah 52:14; 53:3).

Author John Pollock describes the scene as the procession came to the city walls:

> Passing through the Golden Gate of the city, the executioners and those who

followed moved a little way beyond the walls
to where the ground began to rise to the
western hill overlooking Jerusalem. They
stopped on a rocky outcrop with contours
which fitted its name, Place of the Skull
(*Golgotha* in Aramaic, *Calvarius* in Latin)."[5]

Before them stood the stark tree trunks and pot-
holes from previous executions. It was an eerie and ugly
place. Gravel pits, tombstones, and the clutter of the
city were strewn about. There, in this awful place, Jesus
was nailed to the cross, along with two others who were
condemned to die.

The soldiers laid the prisoners on the cross beams
and tied them down. Then they picked up the long iron
spikes, raised their hammers, and began to pound. They
drove the spikes through the wrists of the victims,
pinning their arms to the cross.

The steady crack of the hammers could be heard
above the screams of the victims and the cries of their
relatives. Each blow increased the pain. Each strike of
the hammers told the condemned that there was no
hope of release.

But as the hammers rang out against the rocky cliff,
one steady voice could be heard above the clamor and
the pain.

"Father, forgive them; for they know not what they
do" (Luke 23:34 KJV).

Even in this awful moment, Jesus would rise above
it all. Here at The Place of the Skull we see no squirming,
squealing victim—no angry, cursing man. We see the
Savior in all His greatness, goodness, and compassion.
We see Him forgiving His unsuspecting executioners.

Let the hammers ring! For in their ugly sound we
hear the grace of God shouting above them all. From

the very throne of God, through the canyon of eternity, comes the one word of hope for all mankind—*grace!*

Grace that is greater than all our sin. Wonderful, marvelous, matchless grace, flowing from the heart of God. Grace, reaching out across the cavern of time, planned from the dawn of history before the worlds were ever framed.

This was the moment of divine triumph, the ultimate and final victory over sin. The Son of God Himself was nailed to a cross, bearing our sins and taking the curse. He had become the Lamb of God, slain for the sins of the world.

Picture Him there if you can. And ask yourself: Has there ever been anyone like Him? Is there any other Savior who deserves my life, my love, my worship? Is there anyone to compare with Jesus? Is there anyone who loves like He loves? Is there anyone who cares like He cares?

Michael Green writes, "The physical effects of crucifixion were appalling. Of all deaths, it is the most lingering and agonizing."[6] The unnatural position of the body, its suspension on jagged nails, the excruciating pain, the raging thirst, the open wounds—together they ravaged the gaping victim.

Crucifixion was intended to be cruel. It was the most horrible thing the Romans could think to do. The victim was literally tortured to death. In time, sheer physical exhaustion set in. The loss of blood and the victim's constant pulling up of his body weight against the nails finally took him. Too tired to pull any longer, he slumped forward, hands limp, heels bloodied against the base of the cross, head dropped. Slowly, he choked to death. And then it was over.

Some men kept up this hideous ritual for days before they died. The average was about 24 hours. If the victim remained alive too long, the soldiers would break his legs so he would be unable to push and pull any longer.

Jesus didn't last 24 hours. Within just six hours, He was dead. There was no need to break His legs. The spear thrust into His side told the story—blood and water. Medical doctors have long observed the meaning: He died of a broken heart. The weight of our sin came down upon His soul in those final moments on the cross, and His heart exploded.

Isaiah foresaw this as well when he wrote:

> He was pierced for our transgressions,
>   he was crushed for our iniquities;
> the punishment that brought us peace was
>       upon him,
>   and by his wounds we are healed.
> We all, like sheep, have gone astray,
>   each of us has turned to his own way;
> And the LORD has laid on him
>   the iniquity of us all (Isaiah 53:5-6).

In those awful moments, Jesus was rejected by men and forsaken by God. But in those same moments He defeated sin and death for all who would believe in Him. He paid the supreme price and took the full fury of the wrath of God. In so doing, He transformed the cross from a symbol of shame to one of glory.

Something as ugly as a cross became the symbol of a dynamic new faith. Something so despised by the world became the hope of every believer. Why? Because the cross was touched by Jesus' presence, and from that time onward it was never the same.

No wonder Isaac Watts wrote:

## Let the Hammers Ring!

When I survey the wondrous cross
On which the Prince of Glory died,
My richest gain I count but loss,
And pour contempt on all my pride. ❋

# 11
~

# It Is Finished!

> When he had received the drink, Jesus
> said, "It is finished." With that he
> bowed his head and gave up his spirit.
>
> John 19:30

The cross was the climax of history. Then and
there God settled the issue of our salvation. At The
Place of the Skull the sin debt was paid once for all.

When Jesus died there in our place, He took the
punishment that we deserved. He received the full fury
of the wrath of God. Yet, He came away victorious.
And so did we.

This was no mere bookkeeping transaction. It
was a personal transaction between the Father and the
Son. The Father put our sins upon the Son so that He
actually became sin for us. He became the curse and
bore the agony of hell. He got what we deserved.

R.C. Sproul observes:

> On the cross Jesus does not merely
> receive the curse of God. He becomes the
> curse. He is the embodiment of the

curse. . . . The cross represents the great suffering of Christ. The suffering far transcends physical pain. It is more than a human death; it is an atonement. Christ is the sacrificial lamb. He must bear the weight of divine displeasure. He must feel the wrath of the Father poured out against sin."[7]

This is the heart of the gospel. It is the good news that Christ died for sinners. He took our place and did for us what we could not do for ourselves—He paid for our sins.

John Stott expresses it like this: "Moved by the perfection of his holy love, God in Christ substituted himself for us sinners."[8] In that moment, all of human history changed. A new day dawned—the day of salvation. A new relationship was established—the bride of Christ. And a new hope was born—eternal life.

To those who stood near the cross, it seemed like the end. Jesus, the Messiah, the Savior, was dead. He had breathed His last. His body hung limp, still fastened by the nails.

Just before He died, Matthew tells us that He shouted with a loud voice (27:50). John tells us *what* he shouted: "It is finished" (19:30). It was a shout of triumph, not a whimper of defeat. It was the pronouncement of victory that always came at the end of the Day of Atonement, and every Jew recognized it. When the sacrifice was completed and after the scapegoat had been driven out of their midst, the people shouted, "It is finished."

The Greek New Testament uses the term *tetelestai*, which can be translated "paid in full." The atonement was complete, the penalty paid. And our eternal destiny was sealed.

The Bible tells us that during those awful moments when God's wrath fell upon His Son, "darkness came over all the land" (Matthew 27:45). Christ was left alone, like a forsaken sinner, to suffer and die in our place.

Almost everything we do in our churches reflects upon what was accomplished on the cross. Our hymns of praise thank God for His eternal salvation. Our sermons are filled with appeals to come to the Savior. Our testimonies recount His grace and goodness in our lives. Our church architecture usually includes a cross—a visible reminder of the Savior and the salvation He offers.

But it is the *empty* cross that reminds us best. He is not still suffering; He is no longer dying. He is alive! The cross is empty. And so is the tomb. He is not here; He is risen just as He said.

Jesus was executed in a remote corner of the Roman Empire, in a city that was later totally destroyed. His disciples forsook Him. One denied Him. Another betrayed Him. Yet, shortly after His death, they reemerged, proclaiming that He was alive.

In a short period of time a dynamic new religious faith arose. Within 30 years that faith had spread to the great cities of the Roman Empire, spread by the very disciples who had failed to stand with Jesus at His hour of execution.

Even more incredible was the central figure of this new faith: Jesus Christ, a Jewish carpenter, who had been *crucified!* This was beyond comprehension in the Roman world. Only criminals, slaves, and terrorists were crucified. The cross was the most ugly and dreaded symbol in the empire.

But Jesus changed all that. He took the worst and made it the best. He transformed the very meaning of the cross. *He* went to the cross. *He* died on the cross. *He* paid for our sins on the cross. And *He* triumphed on the cross.

Today, we wear the cross as jewelry. We decorate our churches with it, make lapel pins of it, design our buildings in its shape, and display it in our stained-glass windows. That which was a sign of ridicule, rejection, and pain has become the shining symbol of our salvation.

But the cross is more than a symbol. It is a reminder of what the Savior did there for us. He took our sins upon Himself so that He might change us. He didn't come to change the symbol; He came to change us. He came to redeem us from the curse of the Law, from the wrath of God, and from the condemnation of the devil.

*And He succeeded!* That's the good news. His death was not defeat; His crucifixion was not the end. It was the beginning. The beginning of our salvation. What was finished on the cross would continue to bloom again and again in the hearts of those who would receive Him as their Savior.

Theologians call it "the finished work of Christ." He completed all that He set out to accomplish. He took our place, paid for our sins, and won a great victory on our behalf. He settled the matter of our eternal destiny and secured for us a home in heaven.

All other biblical doctrines revolve around this central theme: Christ died for our sins according to the Scriptures. His triumph is our triumph. His victory is our victory. His success is our success.

The apostle Paul said it this way: "In all these

things we are more than conquerors through him who loved us" (Romans 8:37).

The key to understanding the cross is love. God loved us so much that He sent His Son to die in our place. He loved us so much that He would not hold back sending our judgment upon Him. And Jesus loved us so much that He took it—all of it. For us.

That is why Charles Wesley could write:

> Amazing love! How can it be
> That thou, my God, shouldst die for me?[9] ✳

# 12

## The Party's Over

*Joseph took the body, wrapped it in a clean linen cloth, and placed it in his own new tomb that he had cut out of the rock. He rolled a big stone in front of the entrance to the tomb and went away.*

Matthew 27:59-60

Have you ever wondered what happened during those three days Jesus was in the tomb? Imagine the agony of Jesus' family and the disappointment of the disciples. All their hopes and dreams were crushed in those dark hours.

The crucifixion had ended with the jolt of an earthquake and a period of intense darkness. It was as if God turned off the lights of the whole planet for awhile. His Son had been rejected and His enemies had turned the whole miserable ordeal into a kind of party.

"He saved others," they said, mocking, "but he can't save himself!" Even one of the thieves crucified with Jesus hurled insults at Him. One of the tragedies of hanging on a cross was the public humiliation of it all.

There was no place to hide. You could see and hear everything being said about you.

After a few hours, probably from 9:00 A.M. until noon, God said, "Enough! Turn out the lights. The party's over." And from noon until 3:00 P.M., the Bible says "darkness came over the whole land . . . for the sun stopped shining" (Luke 23:44-45).

It was also during this time that the veil inside the Temple was torn from top to bottom. The veil was a heavy curtain that separated the Holy of Holies from the rest of the Temple. It set off the sacred room where the Ark of the Covenant once sat.

The curtain signified that sinful man could not come into a holy God's presence. Its rending during the earthquake symbolized that man now had access to God because of what Jesus had accomplished on the cross.

No longer would we have to be kept at a distance. From now on, every believer would have direct access to God. In the book of Hebrews we are told, "Since we have confidence to enter the Most Holy Place by the blood of Jesus, by a new and living way opened for us through the curtain . . . let us draw near to God with a sincere heart in full assurance of faith" (10:19-22).

So intense was the darkness that covered Golgotha that day that people trembled. The crowd was terrified. Many left and hurried home in fear. Matthew 27:52 tells us the earthquake shook the nearby tombs and that Old Testament saints arose and appeared to many people in Jerusalem.

We cannot fully comprehend all that took place in those few hours. The redemption of mankind was sealed. Satan was defeated. The curse was reversed. The old dispensation came to an end.

The rending of the curtain in the Temple also signified the end of the old covenant. Animal sacrifices were now obsolete. The Lamb of God had died for the sins of all mankind. Daily sacrifices were no longer necessary. In a few short years the Temple itself would be removed. The old religion would be replaced by a "new and living way."

The tearing of the curtain also revealed an ugly fact. The lights were out in the Holy of Holies. God had departed centuries before, even before the Babylonians destroyed the first Temple. This second Temple, though greatly remodeled and expanded by Herod, never had the glory resident within it.

Now, every priest in the Temple could see the darkness for himself. There was no glory within that sacred room. The glory was out there at Calvary, hanging on a cross! No wonder so many priests would later come to believe that Jesus was the Savior. They had been exposed to the emptiness of the sacred room. They had seen for themselves that God was not there.

Surely the Temple priests put up another curtain and tried to explain away the whole incident. They probably even made the area "off limits" for awhile. But it was too late. The damage was done. It was dark in the Holy of Holies, and every priest knew it.

Back on Calvary's hill, Jesus breathed His last. "Father, into your hands I commit my spirit." He bowed His head and released His spirit.

Jesus' every action was voluntary. He had not died as a martyr, a victim of circumstance, or even as a moral example. He willingly accepted death as the substitutionary Lamb of God. He was dying in our place, with our sins upon Him.

The whole event was so overwhelmingly powerful that the Roman centurion who stood at the base of the cross was filled with amazement. All he could say was, "Surely he was the Son of God!" (Matthew 27:54).

Jesus hung lifeless on the cross while the soldiers picked up iron mallets to break the legs of the thieves. It was one last act of cruelty. Sunset was coming, the Sabbath would begin, and nobody could defile the Sabbath. The bodies had to come down. But first, the victims had to die. By breaking their legs, the soldiers rendered them helpless to push and pull against the nails and the thieves would soon choke to death.

John Pollock describes the deadly scene: "As the evening shadows lengthened, John watched, numbed with sorrow, the gruesome work of extracting the nails with iron pincers, lowering rigid arms, and laying the corpse on the ground."[10]

John took Mary to the home of John Mark, who lived in the city. Some of the other women remained at the site of the crucifixion and sat there in stunned silence. Joseph of Arimathea, a wealthy disciple, went to Pilate, along with Nicodemus, and secured permission to bury Jesus' body. They embalmed it with spices, wrapped it in linen, and carried the body to the tomb in Joseph's garden nearby.

Mary Magdalene and her companions followed the men to the tomb and sat in brokenhearted silence while the body was laid on the rock-hewn shelf inside. After they emerged from the tomb, some servants rolled the heavy stone over the opening. And Jesus was gone from view. It was all over. The group finally returned to the city at nightfall.

Pollock again describes the scene: "John, Mary, and the other women spent the night and day of the Sabbath in mute despair. Their world had collapsed. Neither the ancient prophets nor the recent words of Jesus could penetrate their grief. Bereft of him, they had lost hope and purpose."[11]

Jesus was gone. And with Him, all hope had vanished. We can only attempt to imagine the agony of the disciples during that awful night, the long Sabbath, and the early hours of Sunday morning.

The Lord's body lay cold in the grave. But Jesus Himself? You can't kill a spirit. And you surely can't kill God! Where was He? Busy about His Father's business.

First Peter 3:18-20 explains what happened during those hours in the tomb: "He was put to death in the body but made alive by the Spirit, through whom also he went and preached to the spirits in prison who disobeyed long ago."

Ephesians 4:7-10 explains that before Jesus ascended into heaven, He descended to the "lower, earthly regions." The Apostles' Creed says, "He descended into hell." He suffered the punishment of hell on the cross, but then He descended into hell itself. He even preached there.

Why would Jesus preach in hell? Its residents are lost and condemned forever with no hope of salvation. So what did He have to say to Satan, demons, and the lost?

"The party's over!"

Jesus descended into hell to announce the ultimate triumph of His death on the cross, a triumph which sealed the fate of believers and unbelievers alike.

If Satan thought for one moment the crucifixion was a victory for the hordes of darkness, Jesus banished all his hopes. It marked Satan's ultimate defeat and Jesus' ultimate victory.

While the disciples wept, the Savior conquered hell itself. He descended into the lair of the devil, and Satan could not touch Him, claim Him, or hold Him.

Jesus' proclamation, "It is finished" echoed through the caverns of hell. Satan was helpless to prevent Him access. The father of lies had been exposed by the truth. And then Jesus went to Paradise—"Abraham's bosom" it was often called—and took the souls of the Old Testament saints to heaven.

"He ascended on high, [and] he led captives in his train," the Scripture explains (Ephesians 4:8-9; cf. Psalm 68:18). Those Old Testament saints who came out of their graves during the crucifixion eventually went on to glory—to heaven itself—to await the arrival of New Testament believers. They are there now, waiting for us.

That's what happened during the three days Jesus was in the tomb. Three days that changed the world—and it was just a small preview of what was to come. ✳

# 13

## When Empty Means Extraordinary

*There was a violent earthquake, for an angel of the Lord came down from heaven and, going to the tomb, rolled back the stone and sat on it.*

Matthew 28:2

The resurrection is the ultimate proof that Jesus is the Son of God. It is the strongest argument for the truth of Christianity. It separates Jesus from all other religious leaders. He is not just a great teacher; He is a risen Savior!

The resurrection of Jesus Christ is the most unique event in all the world. There is nothing else to compare to it. First, He is the only person to raise Himself from the dead. Second, He is the only person ever raised who did not later die a natural death.

Jesus rose from the dead and is alive evermore. That is why the Bible refers to Him as "the firstborn from among the dead" (Colossians 1:18). He is first in priority over all those who will one day be raised to life again. In fact, His resurrection is proof that He does indeed have the power to raise us to life.

Critics of the Christian gospel are hard-pressed to discount the resurrection story. There were so many eyewitnesses. Every one of the disciples eventually sealed his testimony with his life. Each one died a martyr, claiming the message was true.

Then there are all the personal aspects of the story. The despair of the disciples. The confusion among the women who found the stone rolled away. The panic of the Jewish leaders. The embarrassment of the Roman officials. The insistence of the Roman officials. The assertion by Thomas that the others were deceived.

No one inventing such a tale would have told it the way it was told. *Women* saw Him first? Their testimony wasn't even admissible in a first-century court of law. The body was *missing*...from a guarded tomb? His disciples were telling everyone He was alive? Who could believe those cowards?!

The story itself is intriguing. Consider the details. The disciples and the women passed the Sabbath in secrecy. This was no time to be seen in public, walking about. But when Sunday morning came, even before sunrise, Mary Magdalene and the other women prepared spices to finish anointing the hastily buried corpse.

But as they walked toward the tomb in the early morning dawn, they wondered who would help them remove the stone. It is generally estimated that it weighed about two tons. In addition, the high priest had secured permission to station a contingent of guards at the tomb and Pilate had authorized the sealing of the stone.

When the women finally arrived at the tomb, they were surprised to see that the stone was already rolled away. The guards had fled. And the body was gone!

Mary Magdalene was overcome with grief. "They have taken the Lord out of the tomb, and we don't know where they have put him!" she cried (John 20:2). She seems to have assumed that the Jewish or Roman officials had moved the body and she raced back to tell the disciples.

Peter and John ran to the tomb in panic. They found the burial shroud and the facial cloth, but the body was gone. Then they went to tell the others. John seems to be the only one who believed it might have been a miracle. The others were still in deep despair. They knew what crucifixion meant—certain death. They wanted to believe, but they couldn't.

What happened to the body? Frank Morrison, a British journalist and former skeptic, stated it best in his volume titled, *Who Moved the Stone?*[12] Based on the evidence in the Gospel accounts, the stone was moved and the body was missing. The options are limited as to who moved the stone:

1. The women—too weak.

2. The disciples—too afraid.

3. The Jews—no possibility.

4. The Romans—why bother?

5. Grave robbers—not likely.

6. The guards—inconceivable.

Matthew 28:2 gives the only valid explanation: The "angel of the Lord came down from heaven . . . and rolled back the stone." Why? To let Jesus *out*? No, He was already gone! The angel rolled away the stone to let us *in* so we could see for certain that the Savior was no longer there. If Jesus' resurrected body could vanish through the graveclothes and later appear inside walled rooms, He certainly could vanish through the stone walls of the tomb.

The ultimate proof of Jesus' resurrection came Sunday night. Ten of the disciples were assembled in the Upper Room. Thomas was missing; Judas was dead. But the others were there when Jesus suddenly appeared.

Eveyone was stunned. They weren't used to seeing Jesus appear to them in this manner. Some people even thought He was a ghost.

"Why are you troubled?" Jesus asked. "Look at my hands and my feet. It is I myself! Touch me and see; a ghost does not have flesh and bones, as you see I have" (Luke 24:38-39). He even proceeded to eat a piece of fish to show them that He was real. Oh, He was different—He could appear and disappear—but He was real. Very real.

Next, Jesus sat down and taught them the Hebrew Scriptures. He showed them all the prophecies that pointed to Himself. The Bible says, "He opened their minds so they could understand the Scriptures" (Luke 24:45). How did they know which prophecies were about Christ? Jesus Himself taught them, verse by verse.

The only problem with that wonderful evening was that Thomas wasn't there. When the ten told Thomas that they had been with the Lord, Thomas wouldn't believe it. This incident adds credibility to the resurrection story; it affirms that the disciples were firmly convinced Jesus was truly dead. They just couldn't buy the resurrection without seeing Him for themselves.

"Unless I see the nail marks in his hands and put my finger where the nails were," Thomas told them, "and put my hand into his side, I will not believe it" (John 20:25).

Who could blame Thomas? The resurrection sounded too good to be true. Perhaps the disciples just *thought* they saw Him. But . . . there was that part about touching Him and watching Him eat. And the Bible study around the table. Still, it just couldn't be . . . could it?

One week later, Jesus appeared to all the disciples, Thomas included. The doors were locked, the disciples were assembled, and Jesus appeared instantly in the room.

"Peace be with you!" the Savior announced.

It was Him! Really Him!

Then Jesus turned to Thomas. He looked right at him, held out His nail-scarred hand, and said, "Put your finger here; see my hands. Reach out your hand and put it in my side."

Thomas was totally overcome. He fell at Jesus' feet and cried, "My Lord and my God!" There was no doubting this time. He knew Jesus was alive. He had seen Him for himself!

"Because you have seen me, you have believed," Jesus said. "Blessed are those who have not seen and yet have believed."

That's where we come in. We have not actually seen the risen Christ, even though ours is a faith based upon facts. Those facts are clearly expressed in the Gospel accounts and were so convincing that thousands of people living at the time came to believe them and to pass them on to us.

We, too, must consider those facts. Someone rolled away the stone. The body was missing, and no one ever produced it to counter the claims of resurrection. The disciples, hundreds of them, claimed to have seen the risen Christ (*see* 1 Corinthians 15:6). Most of them were still living when the apostles were evangelizing the world, writing the Gospels, and distributing their epistles. Anyone could certainly have checked out the story for themselves.

If the people who lived closest to the event believed it, how much more should we believe it! Time

has not invalidated their testimony; it has only rein-
forced its truth. For 2000 years people have anchored
their eternal destiny on the hope that Jesus is alive. And
for 2000 years people have found a dynamic faith in a
living Savior.

If Jesus really rose from the dead, He is the greatest
person who ever lived. If He is actually alive today, He
is a living Savior. He, and He alone, can grant eternal
life, because He, and He alone, is the author of life.

"I am the resurrection and the life," He said. "He
who believes in me will live, even though he dies" (John
11:25). What a claim! There is no greater promise. And
there is no greater Lord. ✻

# 14

## The Last Breakfast

*esus said to them, "Come and have breakfast." . . . This was now the third time Jesus appeared to his disciples after he was raised from the dead.*

John 21:12,14

Breakfast with Jesus. Wouldn't that be great? At a seaside setting on the lake in Galilee in the fresh morning air. What fellowship! What an opportunity!

John 21 records this appearance of the risen Savior sometime after the appearances in the Upper Room in Jerusalem. For 40 days, the Lord continued to make such appearances prior to His ascension to heaven.

On this occasion Peter, Thomas, James, John, Nathanael, and two others were back in Galilee. We get the impression they were still unsure of what to do as they waited for some word from the Savior.

"I'm going out to fish," Peter announced to the others.

"We'll go with you," they replied.

It was a natural enough choice. Most of them had fished all their lives. So they got into a boat and off they went. They fished all night, but caught nothing.

How embarrassing. They were supposed to be professionals. But they had been away from the business the better part of the last three years, tramping around the countryside with Jesus. Maybe they had lost their touch?

By morning, a strange figure appeared on the shore. They were still about 100 yards away and they couldn't make Him out in the morning haze.

"Friends, haven't you any fish?" He called to them.

"No," came back their embarrassed reply.

"Throw the net on the right side of the boat," the stranger suggested.

When they did, the nets were instantly filled—just like the miracle years earlier in Luke 5.

"It is the Lord!" John exclaimed.

Peter couldn't believe it. There he sat in his underwear. Quickly, he grabbed his outer garment, dove into the water, and swam ashore, leaving the six others to wrestle with the net full of fish.

When they all got to the beach they found that Jesus had prepared breakfast for them. John records three elements that Jesus provided: bread, fish, and a fire of coals.

"Bring some of the fish you have just caught," the Savior suggested.

Peter wanted to do anything he could to please the Master; the guilt of those three denials still weighed heavily upon him. So he ran to the boat and dragged the net full of fish himself.

"Come and have breakfast," the Lord said to them.

Here is the risen Christ eating a meal with the disciples. Perhaps it suggests that eating food will be part

of our heavenly experience. Fellowship with the risen
Christ is certainly a present reality; in the communion
service, we celebrate His death and resurrection until
He comes again.

As they gathered around the fire, Jesus took the
fish and the bread, broke and multiplied them, and
distributed them to the disciples—just like He had done
at the feeding of the 5000, which had occurred nearby.
This was the last miracle they would ever see Him do.

When they finished the meal, Jesus turned to Peter.
It was time to clear up the matter about the three
denials. They were still huddled around the fire when
the first question came—just as Peter had huddled
around the fire in the courtyard of the high priest's
palace. He could not have missed the obvious parallel.

"Simon," Jesus said, using Peter's predisciple name,
"do you truly love me more than these?" the Savior
asked.

More than what—these other disciples? Remember,
Peter had protested at the Last Supper that he loved the
Lord more than the other disciples.

But this time Peter was cautious. He was a broken
man and wasn't about to overstate his devotion. He
surely wasn't going to position himself above the others.

Twice Jesus would ask if Peter loved Him, using the
Greek word *agapao*. It was the highest possible word for
love. But each time, the humbled fisherman would reply,
"Yes, Lord, you know that I love you," using the Greek
word *phileo*. It was often interchangeable in its usage
with *agapao*, but it reflected a lesser form of love.

Finally, Jesus asked a third time, "Do you love me?"
This time, the Greek text uses *phileo* both in the
question and in the answer. Much has been said by
commentators on the interplay between the two words,
but one thing is obvious.

Peter had denied Jesus three times, and three times Jesus asked him to reaffirm his love for Him. For each denial there was an affirmation. For the emotion-packed third denial, there was an emotion-filled third affirmation.

To each response of fidelity, Jesus told Peter to serve Him: 1) feed My lambs; 2) take care of My sheep; 3) feed My sheep. Again there is an interchange of terms, this time between lambs and sheep. But the overarching principle is the same: Go and serve My church.

Restoration is difficult. It requires true repentance on the part of the offender and true grace on the part of the offended. It cannot be granted easily, as though the offense were not serious. Nor can it be withheld, as though forgiveness were not possible.

Jesus could forgive Peter because He had already died for his sins. He could restore him to service because He was the risen, living Lord of the church. He was calling the shots and making the decisions, and He had decided to call Peter back into His service.

Those who have never failed like Peter have a tendency to misunderstand restoration. Why should Jesus give such people another chance? What could they possibly do for Him? Why would He even want them?

But those who have failed clearly understand. They have been to the bottom. They have come to the end of themselves and they realize something we all need to realize: We are all failures in God's eyes.

Every one of us has fallen short. Even as believers, we have not been what we should have been or what we could have been. There is something of Peter in all of us—pride, arrogance, spiritual blindness. Failure.

None of us deserves to serve Him. He is so much greater than we will ever be. He is holy and we are sinful. He is God and we are human. But He is also the Savior. He is in the business of restoring old wrecks and rekindling cold hearts.

The Savior is calling: "Do you love Me? Then go and serve Me."

When knowledge of our repentance exceeds the knowledge of our sin, we are ready to be restored to His service. ✳

# 15

~

# Friends in
# High Places

*T herefore, since we have a great high
priest who has gone through the heavens,
Jesus the Son of God, let us hold firmly
to the faith we profess.*

Hebrews 4:14

Forty days after the resurrection, Jesus led the
disciples to the Mount of Olives. There, on the crown
of the hill, above Gethsemane, He told them to wait in
Jerusalem for the fulfillment of the Father's promise.

"You will receive power when the Holy Spirit
comes on you," He promised. "And you will be my
witnesses in Jerusalem, and in all Judea and Samaria,
and to the ends of the earth" (Acts 1:8).

Then something happened. He had warned them
that it would, but still they weren't ready for it. He
began to ascend into the clouds, higher and higher until
He disappeared. This time He was gone for good.

The disciples stood there, gazing up into the
clouds. Silent. Stunned.

"Why do you stand here looking into the sky?"
two men (presumably angels) asked them. "This same

Jesus, who has been taken from you into heaven, will come back in the same way you have seen him go into heaven" (Acts 1:11).

In this one incident we have two great parameters in Jesus' present ministry: from the *ascension* to the *second coming*. The question is, What is He doing in the meantime?

First, Jesus ascended to the Father, back to the glory that He had with Him from all eternity. In fulfillment of His priestly prayer in John 17, Jesus returned to His original glorified state.

That is why He looked so different when He appeared to John 60 years later on the Isle of Patmos in Revelation 1:12-20. John described Him as one "like a son of man," dressed in a high priest's robe with a "golden sash" around his chest. Then the beloved disciple writes, "His head and hair were white like wool, as white as snow, and his eyes were like blazing fire."

Jesus looked so different, like He did at the Transfiguration. John could not stand before Him and fell at His feet like a dead man. But then the Savior touched him.

"Do not be afraid," He said. "I am the First and the Last. I am the Living One; I was dead, and behold I am alive forever and ever!"

Jesus Christ today is the ever-living, glorified Son of God. He is Lord of the church, moving among His people, regenerating their lives by His Spirit, and empowering their service in His kingdom. To Him, all heaven sings, "Worthy is the Lamb."

We worship Him because of who He is and because of what He has done. He is the Savior. And there is no other.

The Book of Hebrews describes our Lord's present high-priestly ministry. He is called our "great high priest" (4:14), who is able to sympathize with our weaknesses (4:15), and who represents us to the Father (5:1), with prayers and petitions bathed in tears (5:7).

Unlike earthly priests who must offer sacrifices for their own sins, Jesus is our sinless Savior (4:15b; 5:3). Unlike human priests who eventually die, Jesus is our eternal priest (7:24). He sits at the right hand of the Almighty (8:1) and serves in the Temple of heaven itself (8:2).

He is the executor of a new covenant, made in His own blood. For "without the shedding of blood there is no forgiveness" (9:22). On the basis of that shed blood, He can enter heaven itself, "now to appear for us in God's presence" (9:24). His is an ongoing ministry on our behalf. He has chosen to represent us to the Father and He will continue to represent us for all eternity.

Unlike human priests who had to stand up continually to make their sacrifices, Jesus Christ, God's High Priest, has offered one sacrifice—Himself! For all time. He is now seated at the right hand of the Father in heaven (10:12). His sacrificial ministry is complete, yet His intercessory ministry is continual.

What does that mean to us? It means that we can come boldly into the presence of God. Hebrews 10:21-22 says, "Since we have a great priest over the house of God, let us draw near to God with a sincere heart in full assurance of faith."

That means that you do not have to be afraid of coming to God. Jesus paved the way with His own blood and you do not have to hesitate to follow Him, right up to the throne of God.

Come! Not because you deserve to come, but because Jesus bids you come. He makes it possible for you to come just as you are.

The Bible describes our Lord's present ministry not only as a High Priest, but also as a heavenly defender. First John 2:1 refers to our Lord as the "one who speaks to the Father in our defense." He functions as our defense lawyer in heaven.

The biblical term used here *paraclete,* or "advocate." Jesus has not only saved us from the penalty of sin by His past action on the cross, but He also continues to save us from the power of sin by His present action in heaven.

While Satan delights in accusing our every failure before the Father, we have a heavenly defender who pleads His blood on our behalf. He does not argue that we are innocent, because we are not. Rather, He argues that His blood has covered our sins and removed our guilt. We stand acquitted of all crimes against the Father, justified by Christ Jesus.

Charles Spurgeon loved 1 John 2:1. He pointed out that even though we sin as believers, we still have a defender. Sin does not cause us to forfeit our advocate. "All the sin that a believer ever did," he wrote, "or can be allowed to commit, cannot destroy his interest in the Lord Jesus Christ as his advocate."[13]

Notice the designations given to the Savior in 1 John 2:1:

> *Jesus:* Savior—He has the desire to defend us.
>
> *Christ:* Anointed—He has the authority to defend us.
>
> *Righteous One:* Qualified—He has the qualifications to defend us.

Jesus Christ is our perfect defender because He is our perfect Savior. He has been chosen and authorized by the Father as our great High Priest. Therefore, Spurgeon concluded, "We may safely lay our trouble where God has laid His help."[14] The Righteous One is our defender. Jesus Christ the Righteous One: It is not only His name and His nature, but also His plea.

Jesus declares Himself to be our substitute. He credits His obedience and righteousness to our account. He gives us everything we need, even though we don't deserve it. That is what grace is all about. God extends pardon to us beyond our deserving it. He smiles at us and blesses us, even though we don't deserve any of it.

Spurgeon put it like this in one of his sermons: "Come just as you are, all guilty, empty, meritless, and fall before the great King, whom you have so often provoked, and beseech Him of His infinite mercy to blot out your transgressions, to change your nature, and to make you His own. And see if He will cast you away. Is it not written . . . 'Him that cometh to me I will in no wise cast out.'"[15]

That's really what Jesus is all about. He stepped from the glory of heaven to the midnight of earth. He came to rescue us from the kingdom of darkness and bring us into the kingdom of light. He came to save us and transform us. And He continues to preserve us.

Jesus is alive in heaven, serving as our High Priest and heavenly defender. With Him on our side and His Spirit in our hearts, we *will* overcome.

Jesus is doing all of that for you. Because He loves you. There is no greater love because there is no greater Person. And there is no greater hope because there is no greater Savior.

We've got Friends in high places. If God be for us, who can be against us? ✻